**independent Cambridge**

A guide to, and a celebration of,
the City's best independent traders,
venues and events.

PHL
Publishing Limited

**First published in 2012 by PHL Publishing Limited**

© PHL Publishing Limited 2012

**Errors and omissions**

The contents and features in this publication have been compiled and published in good faith. The publisher cannot accept any liability for any claim howsoever arising, including as a result of any person acting or refraining from acting on the contents, and whether any resultant loss is direct or indirect.

**Further copies**

To order a copy of Independent Cambridge 2013 visit www.independent-cambridge.co.uk or email us at info@independent-cambridge.co.uk

Copies also available at bookshops and independents throughout Cambridge.

ISBN-13: 978-0-9574406-0-9

**Cover price £7.99**

## Special offers – only with this book

Why not take advantage of the generosity of some of Cambridge's lovely independents and whenever you see the special offer price tag on one of the feature spreads, use this book to receive a little extra something special when you visit.

Just make sure you have a copy of the book with you!

### Thank you

We, at PHL Publishing would like to say a big thank you to the following people for their help and support in producing this book and generally for their belief in campaigning for independents.

Frances Boyer (couldn't have done it without you Frannie!), Fiona Smith, Polly Plouviez (Urban Larder), Sarah Decent (Modish Shoes), Wendy Howell (Design Essentials), Judy Linford (The Art Department), Toby Bush (The Dog House Solution), Cathy Moore (Wordfest), David Lombari (12a), Kevin Lawrence (Abbeystar Print Solutions), Jessica Prince, Allan Brigham and Caroline Biggs.

# Contents

# Welcome to the first edition of Independent Cambridge

We all love that feeling of stumbling across a funky little boutique selling unique designs, a restaurant or café serving deliciously different food or a piece of work by a new artist which we can't wait to tell friends about. These experiences help us to retain a sense of individuality and connection with other people.

Through words and photographs, Independent Cambridge builds in to a celebratory narrative of this individuality, as well as a showcase for the fantastic range of products, services, venues and events you will only find offered by Cambridge independents.

We also want to turn the spotlight on the owners – whose constant creativity and innovation is keeping the City unique, particularly in difficult times for the British high street. Imagine what it would be like without their stylish and quirky window displays, the huge variety of high quality food (much of which is locally-sourced) and the personal service you only get from shopping independently.

So whether you are a resident of Cambridge or a visitor, we urge you – support our independent traders and events – and we hope this guide will give you an insight in to the best that is available throughout the City. Also, remember to visit www.indpendent-cambridge.co.uk where you can find the only database dedicated solely to independents in Cambridge and the local area.

Finally, we would like to dedicate this book to Suzy Oakes – champion of Mill Road and true supporter of independents everywhere.

*Anne Prince*

Anne Prince
Editor

# Area 1

Castle Street

Northampton Street

Magdalene Street

Thompson's Lane

Bridge Street

St John's Street

All Saints Passage

Trinity Street

# Area 1

*Castle Street, Northampton Street, Magdalene Street, Thompson's Lane, Bridge Street, St John's Street, All Saints Passage, Trinity Street*

Castle Hill is where Cambridge began. The bronze sculpture at the junction of Magdalene Street and Chesterton Lane represents the layers of human habitation archaeologists discovered beneath it, with Roman remains, executed Saxons, and a lost medieval treasure – 1,805 silver pennies and nine gold coins that can be seen in the Fitzwilliam Museum.

'What are the brass studs in the pavement?' is the question most frequently asked by visitors.

The 600 brass studs in the Bridge Street and Magdalene Street pavements represent flowers that you can see carved on nearby college buildings – find the Marguerite above the entrance to St John's.

*Allan Brigham*

# Kettle's Yard

To describe Kettle's Yard – the creation of former Tate Gallery Curator Jim Ede – as an art gallery or a museum or even a collection, is as misleading as just calling it someone's house.

The converted row of once derelict cottages were renovated and transformed to make Jim Ede's house, and it is still home to his fascinating collection of early 20th century British and European paintings, drawings and sculptures as well as carefully chosen items of furniture, natural and man-made objects and books, all beautifully displayed and combined to create a unique (yet at the same time) genuinely 'lived in' environment.

The artists – whose works have been sympathetically arranged alongside pebbles, shells and glass objects in all the rooms of the house from bedrooms to bathrooms and even the attic space – include Ben and Winifred Nicholson, Alfred Wallis, Christopher Wood, David Jones, Joan Miró, Henri Gaudier-Brzeska, Constantin Brancusi, Henry Moore and Barbara Hepworth. The house is also a beautiful setting for a varied music programme with lunchtime concerts, chamber music and new music events and in the gallery next door, is an ever-changing programme of exhibitions of contemporary and modern art.

And probably the most mesmerising aspect of this very special place is the incredible and ever-changing light – enhanced by Sir Leslie Martin's extension, built in the 70s and something you wouldn't expect from what were once designated 'slum cottages' – but something that re-animates Kettle's Yard every time you step inside and really does make every visit different.

**Kettle's Yard**
Castle Street, Cambridge CB3 0AQ
Tel: +44 (0)1223 748100
Email: mail@kettlesyard.cam.ac.uk
www.kettlesyard.co.uk
Tuesday-Sunday and Bank Holiday Mondays
House: (Summer) 1.30-4.30pm (Winter) 2pm-4pm
Gallery: 11.30am-5pm

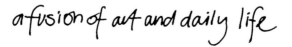

*a fusion of art and daily life*

13

# Cambridge & County Folk Museum

Just a short stroll from the river, past the many independent shops of Magdalene Street and aptly located in the most historic area of the City, is the fascinating and quirky Cambridge & County Folk Museum.

The Museum was founded in 1936 by leading members of the town and University with the aim 'to interest the ordinary citizen in aspects of local social life which were fast disappearing in Cambridgeshire' – an ethos which is still held today.

The museum is housed in a wonderful 17th century, timber-framed building which, for 300 years, was once the White Horse Inn. The rooms of the inn have now been turned in to 'settings', including a bar, a kitchen, the fens and folklore room and a playroom, and each room is packed full of intriguing objects alongside familiar household items – some dating back to the 1600s.

The permanent collection is continuingly being bought to life by the ever-creative temporary displays, events and family activities, some of which provide a genuine 'hands-on' approach to history by using original artefacts, documents and photographs.

The Museum is also home to a shop filled with unique and locally-made toys, gifts and games as well as card and unusual books (great for presents), and a tearoom serving tea and delicious homemade cakes (from local baker, 'Afternoon Tease' on pretty vintage crockery). All proceeds go to supporting the museum.

**Cambridge & County Folk Museum**
2/3 Castle Street, Cambridge CB3 0AQ
Tel: +44 (0)1223 355159
Email: info@folkmuseum.org.uk
www.folkmuseum.org.uk
Tues – Sat: 10.30am-5pm
Sun: 2pm-5pm
Tearoom Sat: 10.30am-4.30pm

*an insight in to the history of Cambridgeshire people*

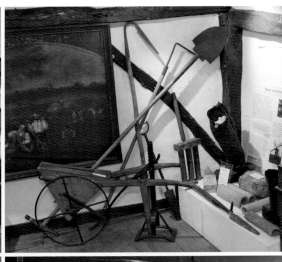

# Chop House Owners: Max, Oliver and Richard

The definition of a chop house – 'a restaurant that serves meat, steak and chops'. Although definitions are useful, in the case of the St John's Chop House and its sister restaurant, The Cambridge Chop House on King's Parade, you need a bit more detail to appreciate the great dining experience that awaits.

The Chop House specialises in traditional and seasonal British cuisine. The menu changes four times a year (seasonally) and although there are similarities between the two locations, different ingredients used by each of the chefs, ensures a fresh take on many of the dishes. And if you are looking for something different, you'll find it at the Chop House. Amongst classics such as steaks, chops, sausages (made on-site) and the ever-popular Beef Wellington, the menu has also featured squirrel, ox cheeks, rabbit and even rook. The game season of late summer/early autumn is particularly suited to the Chop House taste and style. Although an obvious carnivore's dream, the Chop House always has fish and vegetarian options on offer.

So with good food must come good wine and beer! All Cambscuisine restaurants focus their wine lists on the Languedoc-Roussillon region of France. Seven producers, all whom are known personally supply the majority of the wines. Each supplier has been visited by many of the staff in the Languedoc and all suppliers are small independent growers with big passions. Real ales are taken seriously too and are from local suppliers such as Milton and Nethergate breweries, and are all served straight from the cask.

Cambscuisine also owns and runs The Tickell Arms in Whittlesford, The Boathouse in Ely and The Cock at Hemingford Grey, recently awarded the prestigious title of 'Pub of the Year' by the editors of the Good Pub Guide.

**St John's Chop House**
21-24 Northampton Street
Cambridge CB3 0AD
Tel: +44 (0)1223 353110
Email: stjohns@chophouses.co.uk
www.cambscuisine.com

**SPECIAL OFFER**

**Complimentary glass of wine with your meal**

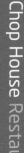

# Primavera Magdalene Street Owner: Jeremy Waller

At the bottom of Castle Hill, on the corner of Magdalene Street and Northampton Street, stands a beautiful listed building. Located in a more intimate setting than its sister gallery on King's Parade, Primavera Magdalene Street is one of Cambridge's hidden pleasures. Step inside, and you will find a quiet haven from the bustling city streets.

Glass and scent bottles by Peter Layton line the windowsills, lending bright accents of colour to catch the eye. Carpets by Jason Collingwood, paintings by Ophelia Redpath and clocks by Julian Spencer create interesting contrasts of texture and form.

The gallery houses Primavera's Artists in Residence and gives Cambridgeshire artists the chance to make the gallery their home and create new work in an inspiring atmosphere. Visitors will enjoy discovering new work and have the chance to personally meet, discover the motivation, and directly support the artists.

This innovative idea from Jeremy, allows artists the opportunity to make use of the space at no charge to them, so the artists profit 100% from their endeavours, while at the same time promoting Primavera, and he is always interested in approaches from new artists who respect Magdalene College's heritage and Primavera's collection and ethos.

Primavera Magdalene Street also displays work by renowned potters Dame Lucie Rie, Hans Coper, Bernard Leach, David Leach, Alan Caiger-Smith, Eric Mellon and Ray Finch. Also on display are ceramics by Peter Hayes, Tony Laverick, Mike Dodds and Sue Binns, cameo glass by Helen Millard and cut glass by Catherine Hough, and paintings by Maz Jackson and Noriko Sasaki (pictured left).

## Primavera

13 Magdalene Street, Cambridge CB3 0AF

Tel: +44 (0)1223 357708

Email: contactprimavera@aol.com

www.primaverauk.com

For opening times, please ring before you visit.

*British artists up close and personal*

# Baska Owner: Baska

Baska is listed as one of the top five Premium Independent Boutiques for 2012. Having recently been nominated for this year's Drapers Fashion Awards, Baska was recognised for its up-to-the-minute sense of fashion and excellent customer service. Established sixteen years ago, this prestigious nomination was well deserved.

From a fabulous dress to the best of everyday wear, Baska ensures that there is something for every occasion. The clothes are all from the top fashion houses such as Moschino Cheap & Chic, Magaschoni and Max Mara. M+F Girbaud and M Missoni can also

be found and with owner Baska's sharp eye for the next trends, new designers are often added to the already brilliant collection. Recently arrived is the new AW12 Faith Connexion collection, fresh from the Paris fashion week.

Alongside the clothes, well-chosen accessories can be found. From the most delicate Otis Jaxon earrings to Red Valentino shoes, striking belts by Marella and a great selection of bags, everything can be provided for that amazing outfit.

A fabulous shopping experience can be found in this shop in Magdalene Street. The light and bright establishment has first-rate facilities for changing and both Baska and her staff are always on hand to give the best advice.

**Baska**
18 Magdalene Street
Cambridge CB3 0AF
Tel: +44 (0)1223 353800
www.baska.co.uk
Mon – Fri: 10.30am-5.30pm
Sat: 10am-6pm

# The Flower House Owner: Sharon Strath

Nestled in one of the most historical, scenic streets in Cambridge sits the most delightful of florists, The Flower House. This well established shop, is proudly one of the top 250 florists in the UK.

Distinctive by its outdoor plants and attractive window display, you will be compelled to walk in; softly lime washed walls create the ideal background for the abundance of flowers. From the exuberant and exotic to the elegant and luxurious the flowers fill the shop with delicious scent.

The ever changing seasons are always represented; autumn and winter incorporate rich shades and vibrant red berries. Perky bright daffodils and delicate snowdrops signal the arrival of spring and then the wonder of sunflowers and sumptuous roses in the summer – inspiration is there at all times of the year. The wonderful selection of flowers are all sourced from the best growers and are always of the highest quality.

The workroom is situated in the middle of the shop and from here all the displays are made up. From wedding and birthday flowers to something to just cheer someone up, advice is always to hand and the staff never tire of talking about flowers. Each individual request can be especially designed for you, and will always be beautifully presented.

The Flower House's focus is to consistently create marvellous combinations for all of life's events.

**The Flower House**
23 Magdalene Street, Cambridge CB3 0AF
Tel: +44 (0)1223 364500
www.theflowerhouse.co.uk
Tues – Fri: 9.30am-5.30pm
Mon & Sat: 8.30am-4.30pm

*Life in flowers*

# Bowns and Bis Owner: Rosalind Bown

Walking along Magdalene Street, as the pavements begin to narrow and the buildings go back in time, there, nestled beneath the eaves of a beautiful 16th century building is Bowns and Bis. The door opens into a large, light and airy room, with rails of gorgeous cocktail dresses, elegant workwear and wedding outfits on every rail. The back of the shop leads you through next door to 'Bis', another delightful room, with weekend clothing, casual shoes and accessories.

The shop is the inspiration of Rosalind Bown: since studying fashion design in London, Rosalind has worked in most aspects of the trade from retail to bespoke tailoring. Bowns and Bis was established fourteen years ago and, thanks to Rosalind's experience and brilliance in interpreting the next season's look, represents everything a shopper could wish for in the search for designer clothes.

Initially championing the 'Best of British' designers, the collection includes Paul Smith, Nicole Fahri and Vivienne Westwood. In among these favourites the selection has now broadened to include the most elegant designers from Paul and Joe and Carven to Schummacher and L'Agence, bringing the most exciting international labels together under one roof.

With Rosalind's professional advice at hand and friendly staff any time spent shopping at Bowns and Bis is a joyous experience.

**Bowns and Bis**
24 & 25 Magdalene Street
Cambridge CB3 0AF
Tel: +44(0)1223 302000
Email: info@bownscambridge.com
www.bownscambridge.com
www.facebook.com/
bownsfashioncambridge
Mon: 10.30am-3pm
Tues –Sat: 10.30am-5.30pm

# Nord Owner: Moira Donald

Whilst studying in Helsinki, Moira Donald was impressed with the simplicity and practicality of Scandinavian design. From furniture to kitchenware, food and clothing, she retained the images until the opportunity arose in 2011 to open Nord.

Appropriately placed on the site of an ancient Viking settlement, Nord's light, calm interior is welcome after the bustle of Bridge Street. The eye is immediately drawn to the display of beautiful interior fabrics designed by the Finnish company, Marimekko. The abstract designs cast shots of colour against the white and neutral backgrounds, creating a vision from the first moment.

The fabrics are complemented by the shelves of delightful ceramics from the Swedish company, Höganäs Keramik, and gleaming glassware from iittala in Finland. Inspiration flourishes as the furniture and lighting are realised, and how the most practical of items, such as shower curtains and coat hooks, can be stylish.

Going through to Café Nord at the back of the shop gives the opportunity to try out some of the Artek and GAD furniture and to sample some delicious Scandinavian fare. The menu is tempting with delights such as fresh rye bread topped with smoked chicken or salmon followed by delicious cakes, all provided by local suppliers, and a good selection of drinks.

**Nord**
36 Bridge Street
Cambridge CB2 1UW
Tel: +44 (0)1223 321884
www.norddesign.co.uk
Mon – Thurs: 10am-5.30pm
Fri – Sat: 10am-6pm
Sun: 11am- 5.30pm

## SPECIAL OFFER

**A free coffee and cinnamon bun in the cafe**

27

# Talking T's

Sitting on the banks of Bridge Street, Talking T's is a fabulous shop that sells the best selection of exclusive hand-printed T-shirts. The business was established over twenty years ago and this creative family have designed most of the prints. The majority of designs give a humorous look at everyday life, emotions and people – "Please wait, sarcastic comment loading" and "Dad, a man with pictures in his wallet where his money used to be", are fine examples!

Sitting alongside these great prints are designs sourced from around the country. Depicting all sorts of things from events in history to zany takes on art, they all entice a smile. Talking T's is also a licensed supplier of the official Cambridge University clothing. This range comes in different styles – T-shirts, polos and sweatshirts – and there is a great range of colours.

Having their own workshop means Talking T's can also supply printed T-shirts for all sorts of events including birthday parties, hen or stag parties or for group holidays and they are happy to print up custom designs. An embroidery service is available for items such as sweatshirts, jackets and polo shirts, and the logo is designed to meet exact requirements. The experienced friendly staff are always on hand to ensure that every occasion has an added element of fun.

**Talking T's**

37 Bridge Street
Cambridge CB2 1UW
Tel: +44 (0)1223 302411
www.t-shirts.co.uk
Mon – Sat: 9.30am-5.30pm
Most Sundays and Bank Holidays: 11am-4pm

# The Varsity Hotel & Spa General Manager: Roberto Pintus

Heading off Bridge Street near the River Cam is Thompson's Lane – an unassuming little street in this historic part of Cambridge. Halfway down the lane and also unassuming from the outside at least, is The Varsity Hotel & Spa.

The Hotel is the vision of a group of Cambridge University graduates and from the moment you step inside, it's obvious they intended to create something quite special in such an historical and beautiful location. Each of the 48 rooms are individually designed and named after Oxbridge Colleges, however if you are now thinking of a traditional, understated look then you would be wrong. Instead, think New York loft meets contemporary English style with incredible views of quintessential Cambridge, and you have The Varsity.

And the higher up you go, the better the views get, until you reach the simply stunning roof terrace with its panoramic view across the Colleges, River Cam and rooftops of Cambridge. Open to hotel and non-hotel guests alike, the terrace also transforms on some evenings in to an open air cinema with large screen as part of the annual Cambridge Film Festival.

More beautiful views of the river can be found at the River Bar Steakhouse & Grill, located just next door and the menu looks pretty good too, with steaks that are dry-aged for a minimum of 28 days and a selection of fish freshly cooked on the grill.

To complete the experience is the Aveda spa, offering customised facials through to hot stone massages. There is also a wonderful Jacuzzi overlooking the Cam with sauna and steam room on hand. A fully-equipped gym and studio with an array of classes are on-site too for the more energetic.

**The Varsity Hotel & Spa**

Thompson's Lane (off Bridge Street)
Cambridge CB5 8AQ

Tel: +44 (0)1223 306030

Email: info@thevarsityhotel.co.uk

www.thevarsityhotel.co.uk

*Boutique chic meets classic Cambridge*

## Petrus Owners: Petra and Steve Slack

If you like your clothes to be design-led rather than necessarily label-led, and you appreciate a genuinely honest and personal approach to customer service, then you should pay Petrus on Bridge Street a visit.

The buying team of Petra, Steve and Faye, is passionate about the use of textures, colours, design and form as well as the comfort and fit of the clothes they choose. These passions are also reflected in the look and feel of the shop too – funky retro-inspired lighting and minimalist fixtures are softened with classic original shop fittings and vintage pieces, all carefully designed and chosen to make visitors feel comfortable – something Petra and her team are particularly good at. In fact, sometimes customers have even bought some of the fixtures, so items in the shop are constantly changing.

A five year stay in Amsterdam for Petra and Steve before setting up Petrus (first in Saffron Walden and now the Cambridge shop), has definitely added a European flavour to their venture. Brands stocked include quirky, Dutch brands Sandwich, whose clothes and accessories for women use unusual and high quality fabrics to create a distinct look, and G Star with a range for both men and women. Another great brand is Cambridge-based fashion company Supremebeing – and Petrus is their only local stockist. With its roots in British street culture, this collection of men's and womenswear combines colour, fit-for-purpose design and attention to detail, all within a stylish and contemporary range that fits perfectly with the Petrus ethos.

**Petrus**
67 Bridge Street,
Cambridge CB2 1UR
Tel: +44 (0)1223 352588
www.facebook.com/petrusdesign
Mon – Sat: 10am-6pm
Sun: 11am-5pm

**SPECIAL OFFER**

**Spend £50 and get 10% off**

# Providence Owners: Kathy and Tim Ritchie

"Have nothing in your homes that you do not know to be useful and believe to be beautiful." This quote by William Morris very neatly sums up all that you will find on a visit to Providence.

Located on the corner of Bridge Street and All Saints Passage, the shop with its lovely, large windows, contains two floors of beautiful, as well as practical, Colonial influenced furniture and other finishing items for the home. Almost 20 years ago, Providence started out as cabinetmakers – producing pieces in oak and pine including freestanding kitchen dressers, larder cupboards and wardrobes. To finish the furniture in the Shaker style, Kathy and Tim developed their own Providence Paint and, as part of

their original shop at Burwash Manor, were also one of the first places in Cambridge to stock paints from the Farrow and Ball range.

As well as the larger pieces of furniture, Providence also houses a selection of Shaker rails, shelves, cabinet hardware and traditional braided rugs. Complementing all this perfectly is an allsorts mixture of equally functional yet cleverly-designed home accessories – from brooms to baskets.

So, returning to the opening quote – why have an everyday potato masher when you can have one in the shape of a daisy from the sculptural Wildflower range by Bojje? Or why use a dreary duster when you can be cleaning the cobwebs away with one fashioned from ostrich feathers? As you can see, along with functionality, Providence combines stylish forms with a dash of vintage, a splash of colour and a great sense of fun.

### Providence

73 Bridge Street, Cambridge CB2 1UR
Tel: +44 (0)1223 506556
www.providenceuk.com
Mon – Fri: 10.30am-5.30pm
Sat: 10am-5.30pm

# Cambridge Craft Market at All Saints Garden

Opposite Trinity College Gatehouse is the historic and beautiful tree-shaded All Saints Garden, once the site of a medieval church. For the last 37 years, dotted amongst the trees surrounding the central memorial cross, a group of local artists and craftspeople gather every Saturday to set up their stalls selling an incredible range of unique handmade items.

A world away from chain-stores and shopping centres, and an independent shopper's heaven, the range of arts and crafts on display is impressive, including photography, jewellery, handmade soaps, bags, hats, scarves, clothes, leather-covered books, pottery, printing blocks, wood turning, wooden place mats, slate picture frames and place mats, wooden animal toys, cakes and drinks, quirky metal figures, embroidery and made-to-order leather belts.

There is no charge to come in to the market and as a number of the artists and craftspeople not only exhibit but also make some of the items there, it's a great opportunity to watch them at work and chat to them about their particular skill. The atmosphere is genuinely friendly, the quality of goods is high and the prices are very reasonable too.

**Cambridge Craft Market at All Saints Garden**
Trinity Street, Cambridge CB2 1TQ
Tel: +44 (0)7769 628788
Email: sugar1972@tesco.net
www.facebook.com/#!/CambridgeCraftMarket
www.cambridge-craft-market.co.uk

Open every Sat all year, plus weekdays (weather permitting) including Fridays in July/August and selected days in the run up to Christmas

*We make what we sell*

# Anthony Owner: Tony Halls

Situated on historic Trinity Street, Anthony has served the discerning gentlemen of Cambridge for over 35 years. For that time, the owner, Tony Halls has focussed on supplying the provincial customer with garments hand-picked from the best Bond Street collections.

Navigating current trends and sourcing only from the best manufacturers, Anthony creates a timeless aesthetic from contemporary shapes and colours. Tailoring from Canali, Pal Zileri and Daks forms the basis of the range, contrasted or co-ordinated with luxury accessories from all over Europe.

Swedish shirt makers Eton supply wrinkle free, Swiss cotton shirts which prove ever popular amongst Cambridge's business class.

For more formal occasions, Anthony hold ranges of black and white tie evening suits including an extensive range of bow ties. Weddings are well-catered for with morning dress, custom made ties and waistcoats.

Made-to-Measure and custom made services are available in both tailoring and shirting which offer an exact fit and a personal touch. Appointments are available during the week until 8pm but must be arranged at least 24 hours in advance.

The experienced staff offer unhurried advice and the fitting and alterations are all part of the exemplary service.

**Anthony**

18 Trinity Street

Cambridge CB2 1TB

Tel: +44 (0)1223 360592

www.anthonymenswear.co.uk

Mon – Sat: 9am-5.15pm

Closed for lunch Mon – Fri: 1pm-1.30pm

18
Anthony
Trinity Street

CANALI

ETON

# Breeze Owner: Anne

This delightful shop in Trinity Street is well worth a visit when looking for an inspired gift or something lovely for the home.

Anne opened her first shop in 1985 selling knits and yarns. Always looking for new ventures, Anne began to incorporate different items. From here she realised that there was a great need for a place specialising in quality gifts and home accessories and so, in 2000, Breeze was opened.

Constantly sourcing new products, Breeze is filled with stylish, innovative and inspirational gifts and items for the home. Walking in is a delight, with shelves full of fun and practical gifts; from cheeky notepads, bicycle bells and old school badges to authentic Cambridge trinkets and all things British, something for everyone and they all come with a guaranteed smile.

The rooms downstairs are inspirational when it comes to buying accessories for the home. Revitalise the bathroom with a brightly coloured soap dish or add some class to the kitchen with beautiful Parlane cookware. Breeze provides a wonderful opportunity to fill your house with gorgeous things and brighten the day.

If it is a party that needs planning, Breeze is the place. Unusual, tiny Chinese balloons and fabulous cupcake cases adorn the shelves alongside little gifts and pretty cake stands – everything that could be wished for to create a stylish occasion.

**Breeze**
34 Trinity Street
Cambridge CB2 1TB
Tel: +44 (0)1223 354403
www.breeze.uk.com
Mon – Sat: 9.30am-5.30pm
Sun: 11am-5pm

**SPECIAL OFFER**

**15% off when you spend over £20.00**

# Cambridge Contemporary Art

It is very easy to feel just a little bit intimidated about stepping in to an art gallery. You really want to go and have a closer look at what's on show, but may be put off by wondering if you will understand it or be able to afford to buy anything on display.

At Cambridge Contemporary Art, in the beautiful and historic Trinity Street, you need not worry about such things. The staff are genuinely friendly and welcoming and more than happy to talk to you about the pieces on show and to tell you about the artists and craftspeople behind the work. Specialising in handmade prints, paintings, sculptures and crafts, the gallery first opened in 1990 and shows the work of over 100 UK-based artists, with a new exhibition every month.

Selected by the Crafts Council for the national list of craft shops and galleries, Cambridge Contemporary Art also makes buying art easy as it's part of the Art Council's Own Art scheme, which is designed to make it easy and affordable to buy original, high-quality contemporary art and craft. You can borrow up to £2,000, or as little as £100, which is paid back interest free in equal instalments over a period of 10 months. The gallery also offers gift vouchers and runs a wedding list service.

Towards the back of the gallery, it's also worth noting, is a fantastic selection of art greetings cards – on sale at a price below the amount asked by most high street card shops. So, as you can see, there really is no reason to feel intimidated by stepping through the door.

**Cambridge Contemporary Art**
6 Trinity Street, Cambridge CB2 1SU
Tel: +44 (0)1223 324222
Email: info@cambridgegallery.co.uk
www.cambridgegallery.co.uk
Mon – Sat: 9am-5.30pm
Sun and Bank holidays: 11am-5pm

# Cambridge University Press Bookshop

Celebrating its 20th anniversary this year, the Cambridge University Press Bookshop is situated in the very heart of historical Cambridge. From the site of number 1, Trinity Street, books have been sold since 1581, making it the oldest bookshop site in the country.

Uniquely, the shop sells books published only by Cambridge University Press; beautiful publications that cover the majority of non-fiction subjects. The ground floor presents new publications, a wonderful section containing local interest titles, shelves of the best-selling Companions series and cases full of books on the humanities and social sciences.

Venturing upstairs, a further wealth of knowledge is contained in the tomes on subjects including classics, law and mathematics, alongside business and management. Theology can also be discovered as well as Cambridge Bibles.

Three years ago saw the opening of the Learning Centre. This covers books for the younger generation with everything from children's books to GCSE and 'A' level revision. There is also a dedicated section for teachers and students of English and state of the art computers where it is possible to try out different learning modules.

Cambridge University Press does not stop at books; with its digital printing, e-publishing and CD roms, the shop is a wonderful mix of history and modern values.

### Cambridge University Press Bookshop

1 Trinity Street, Cambridge CB2 1SZ
Tel: +44 (0)1223 333333
Email: bookshop@cambridge.org
www.cambridge.org/uk/bookshop
Mon – Sat: 9am-5.30pm
Sun: 11am-5pm

# Area 2

Green Street

Sidney Street

Sussex Street

Hobson Street

King Street

# Area 2

*Green Street, Sidney Street, Sussex Street, Hobson Street, King Street*

Oliver Cromwell's head lies opposite Sainsbury's in Sidney Sussex College. Cromwell attended the college as a student, and was MP for Cambridge before becoming Lord Protector after the execution of Charles Ist.

*Allan Brigham*

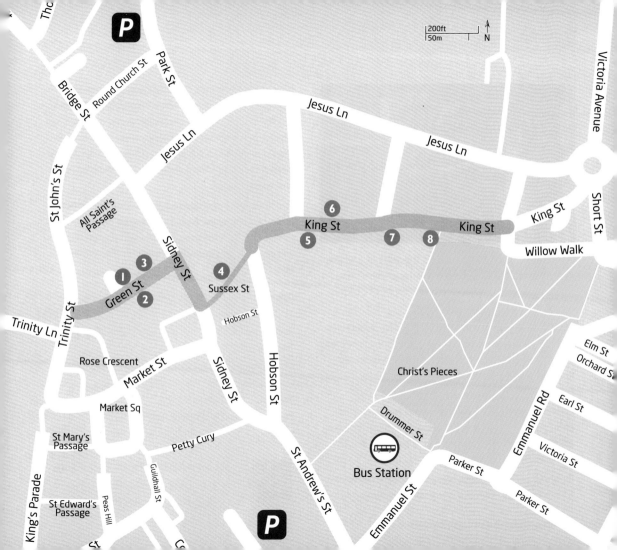

Opening the door to Open Air is the start of a whole new adventure. This boundless independent shop provides everything needed for all types of outdoor activities.

The shop was opened in 1990 by two individuals who combined their knowledge of the outdoor market and the use of equipment in extreme conditions to offer an alternative to the chain store ethic.

Refusing to be saddled with the narrow ranges normally offered, Open Air provides an extensive choice. Alongside European brands such as Bergans of Norway and Fjallraven, they support the British company Rab and many more.

Open Air is divided between three shops. Number 11 contains the splendid range of menswear and outdoor equipment. The adjoining number 12 displays the excellent range of women's clothing; the styles, colours and practicality have all been considered to great effect. A short walk down the road is number 15 where everything is provided for below the knee – from shoes and boots to gaiters and woolly socks.

The long serving, knowledgeable staff are all active users of the products and are able to offer sound advice. The service they provide will ensure that you will embark on your adventure with everything you need.

**Open Air**
11 Green Street
Cambridge CB2 3JU
Tel: +44 (0)1223 324666
Email: enquiries@openair.co.uk
www.openair.co.uk
Mon: 9.30am-5.30pm
Tues – Sat: 9am-5.30pm

## SPECIAL OFFER

**First 20 customers who spend over £50 will be given a Berghaus Limpet daysack value £50.**

# Sundaes

This delightful shop in Green Street specialises in the most stylish of shoes. First established in 1973, this family run business is passionate about shoes and refuses to compromise when it comes to quality or customer service.

Regular visits to the shoe shows in Dusseldorf and Milan ensure that the shop is up to date with the most contemporary of designs from across Europe. Favourite designers such as Think! from Austria are prominent in the shop. The quirky designs in fabulous colours all come with inbuilt comfort.

Sundaes only stock shoes that are made from the best natural materials and highest quality leather. Favourite brands include Arche, Camper, Wonders, Wolky, Paul Green and El Naturalista.

Sitting neatly alongside the shoes is a fabulous range of slippers. Shepherd sheepskin slippers from Sweden will keep your feet cheerful and cosy. Sundaes also has the most comprehensive collection in the country of Haflinger slippers and clogs from Germany. These leather, felt or wool slippers are a delight to put on as soon as you get home.

The shop is well planned and spacious, the displays are uncluttered and large windows provide plenty of light to show the true colours. There is always a good range of sizes in stock and the well trained staff are happy to help.

**Sundaes**
36 Green Street,
Cambridge CB2 3JX
Tel: +44 (0)1223 361536
www.sundaes-shoes.co.uk
Mon – Sat: 9.30am-5.30pm
Sun: 11.30am-4.30pm

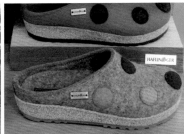

It would be hard not to be tempted by the window display alone, but step inside the door of 3 Green Street and it's instantly obvious why Modish has been recommended by The Guardian as one of the top 100 shoe shops in the UK.

Once you browse the shelves you will discover an incredible range of shoes to suit most budgets but without compromising style or quality. Sarah Decent, the owner of Modish, has travelled extensively to find that perfect mix of popular brands combined with up and coming new talent. So whilst Fly London, Geox, Ruby + Ed, and Vagabond are always

firm favourites at Modish, they also offer a great range of little known designers so there's always something a little bit different from what's offered by the usual high street chains.

This is also reflected in her approach to customer service – Sarah is truly knowledgeable and genuinely believes in only selling good quality, stylish products.

But Modish isn't just about great looking footwear. Because fortunately for the women of Cambridge, Sarah's feet are a sample size 4 – which means she personally tries on everything she buys for the shop. If it's not comfortable, it doesn't make it onto the shelves at Modish, no matter how gorgeous it is.

### Modish

3 Green Street, Cambridge CB2 3JU
Tel: +44 (0)1223 354436
Email: sarah@modishonline.co.uk
www.modishonline.co.uk
Mon – Sat: 9.30am-5.30pm
Sun: 11am-5pm

**SPECIAL OFFER**

**Spend over £30 on shoes and get a free necklace worth £15**

*No pain, no gain? Not at Modish!*

Established eight years ago, The Cambridge Toy Shop is the only independent toy shop in this city. It is a fabulous shop offering a brilliant selection of toys for people of all ages.

Vivienne makes regular trips to the trade fairs in London and Birmingham to ensure that the shop has all the most up-to-date toys and games. For younger children there is so much to see; little kitchens and shops, trains and cars - all there to fuel the imagination and help create their own worlds.

Moving through the shop there is so much to discover – traditional toys such as the beautiful, handmade Merrythought English bears sit well alongside Sylvanian Families and Papo historical figures.

Downstairs, Lego and Playmobil favourites are in constant supply, and there is an amazing array of jigsaw puzzles, board games and modelling kits. Everything from Scrabble and Bananagrams, to Airfix kits and the Think Fun puzzles, there is always something to find and do.

To ensure that everyone gets the most out of their visit to the toyshop, there is a great team of young people working there. Always willing to demonstrate any of the toys on request, their enthusiasm is catching. Weekends will often see face painting and displays going on to make certain that every visit will be fun.

### The Cambridge Toy Shop

15-16 Sussex Street
Cambridge CB1 1PA
Tel: +44 (0)1223 309010
www.cambridgetoyshop.co.uk
Mon – Sat: 9.30am-5.30pm
Sun: 11am-5pm

## Rosie's Vintage Boutique Owner: Carmel

Once upon a day Carmel O'Neill was given a box full of beautiful 1950s dresses by her mother, Peggy. This was the beginning of a career in vintage clothing. Starting at the Vintage Fashion Fairs in London's Hammersmith and Clerkenwell Carmel quickly became a sought after trader, counting among her customers the actor Anna Friel and supplying a number of authentic pieces for the BBC's 1950s drama The Hour.

Building the business by sourcing clothing and accessories from around the world a fabulous vintage collection has evolved. Realising that there was no dedicated vintage clothing shop in Cambridge Carmel decided to bring a little bit of London to this city and opened Rosie's in September 2012.

It would be difficult to walk past the beautiful window display without stopping. Elegant dresses are surrounded by fabulous costume jewellery and satin gloves adorned with intricate beading. Set in a charming period building, inside Rosie's is a lovely light establishment with items spaciously displayed. It is a pleasure to browse the rails and leisurely try the clothes.

The collection includes beautiful vintage bridal gowns and accessories to create a stunning ensemble for a wonderful day. There is exquisite jewellery and wonderful trinkets making it an ideal place for buying extraordinary gifts.

### Rosie's Vintage Boutique

18 King Street, Cambridge CB1 1LN
Tel: +44 (0)7592 359026
www.rosiesvintage.co.uk
Mon – Sat: 10.30am-5.30pm

*It all began with a big cardboard box....*

This unique independent noodle bar has been open for twelve years, during which time it has consistently focused on combining fresh ingredients to create simple yet flavoursome dishes.

The bright, contemporary interior is the ideal setting for this casual Oriental dining experience. The menu offers many delicious appetizers such as spicy squid

and tempura prawns to accompany authentic rice dishes, wok-fried or soup noodles.

Freshly squeezed juices and a good selection of wines and beers, including hot sake and oriental lagers, are available to compliment the food. There are also lunchtime specials available, providing a satisfying meal at a very good price.

Everything is cooked to order and served straight from the open kitchen at the rear of the restaurant. The staff are friendly and always ready to accommodate any dietary requirements or even just to help choose!

**Yippee Noodle Bar**
7-9 King Street
Cambridge CB1 1LH
Tel: +44 (0)1223 518111
www.yippeenoodlebar.co.uk
Mon – Fri: 12noon-3pm and 5pm-10.30pm
Sat – Sun: 12noon-10.30pm

Situated in the centre of King Street, Julian established his hairdressing salon in February 2001. Inspiration came at an early age with his father and uncle both being hairdressers. Whilst studying for his C&G in hairdressing at the Regional College, Julian worked at his father's salon. He went on to work locally for the international company Glemby and was transferred within the company to Selfridge's, London. Opportunities took Julian to Germany where he further developed his skills working in the cities of Mönchengladbach and Dusseldorf.

Situations called him back to Cambridge and, after running his father's salon for a year, he decided to rent a chair at Strands Hairdressers in Victoria Street. Here, Julian built up a loyal client base that has since followed him to his own salon in King Street.

Julian has created a light and comfortable space within a Victorian building, where he specialises in his craft of precision haircuts in classic or contemporary styles. He uses the finest scissors from Japan and the best products available. With 30 years' experience, you can be confident that Julian will create a hairstyle that compliments you.

Julian is passionate about hairstyling and his biggest compliment is his long standing client base that has been an absolute joy to work with. Both women and men of all ages are welcome into his small friendly shop.

**Julian**
56a King Street
Cambridge CB1 1LN
Tel: +44 (0)1223 361644
Mon, Tues, Weds, Fri: 10am-6pm
Sat: 9am-6pm

In April 2009, Keith Wilson opened the doors of Cambridge Strings for the very first time!

As a specialist stringed instrument shop in the very independent King Street area of the city centre, and with over 35 years' experience in music retail, Keith and his colleagues were well-placed to cater for all musicians, from beginners to advanced.

The lovely stock of bowed instruments – new and used violins, violas and 'cellos – are carefully selected (some from local instrument makers) and come in all sizes and price ranges. Cambridge Strings also supplies guitars and ukuleles, with smaller instruments suitable for children, through to the best solid-top guitars, by makers including Admira, Hofner, Yamaha and Martinez.

As well as providing instruments for sale, Cambridge Strings also offers instrument rental services, expert repairs, valuations, servicing and restoration. Cambridge Strings acts at all times as an independent retailer – whose interest is in giving a truly personal service to its customers in a friendly, caring and comfortable environment. The customer

and their satisfaction are always of paramount importance at Cambridge Strings.

The company also offers a wide range of bows (wood or carbon-fibre), bags and cases, all the major brands of strings (including ones for baroque instruments), shoulder and chin rests, resin, tuners, cleaners, dampits, stands and much, much more.

And with an extensive stock of printed music available for teaching, studying and performing for stringed instruments and piano, in all styles, popular and classical, it is clearly a home-from-home for musicians.

### Cambridge Strings

72 King Street, Cambridge CB1 1LN
Tel: +44 (0)1223 323388
Email: sales@cambridgestrings.co.uk
www.cambridgestrings.co.uk
Mon – Sat: 9.00am-5.30pm

# Area 3

# Area 3

*Market Passage, Rose Crescent, Market Street, Market Hill,*
*St Mary's Street, King's Parade, St Mary's Passage, St Edward's Passage,*
*Bene't Street, Trumpington Street.*

The historic Market Square was the centre of commerce and of public life. Until the 1950s this was still the scene of Town and Gown riots every November 5th, a reflection of tensions in the town. As late as 1954 it was reported that homemade bombs were being tossed by the opposing sides and extra police had to be brought in from the County. The November 5th fireworks were moved to Midsummer Common to defuse the situation and today are a much loved family event and the largest annual gathering of residents in the city.

The Corpus clock, on the corner of Bene't Street and King's Parade, is a reminder not to waste time. It features a scary 'chronophage' who eats the hours. Costing £1 million, it was a gift from engineer and inventor John Taylor who said: "I view time as not on our side. He'll eat up every minute of your life and as soon as one is gone he's salivating for the next". Taylor made his fortune from inventing the mechanism that turns off electric kettles once the water has boiled.

The best view in Cambridge is from the top of Great St Mary's tower. Do try it! The tower marks the starting point in 1725 of the first milestones in the country since the Romans times.

*Allan Brigham*

# Ta Bouche

Nestled in amongst the city's most vibrant area is Ta Bouche, sister bar to the fabulous La Raza. The wonderful outdoor seating area on Market Passage gives the bar a marvellous continental feel. Aimed at a younger crowd, Ta Bouche has a unique character and its versatility is outstanding. Whether for brunch, lunch, dinner or drinks, this is the perfect location.

The welcoming ambience is relaxing – the décor is contemporary with walls enriched with black and white photographs. As the day progresses, so does the flow of music. Complemented by the swift service, the volume increases to more energy and fun.

Transcending into nightfall, you can continue with the extensive menu of modern European cuisine. Alongside this are marvellous cocktails – created by the talented bartenders – which can be spontaneous and conjured up to personal specifications. The cocktails are always popular and delight the young people, and all contribute to a good time.

This popular venue has everything you could wish for; its magnetic vibe will entice you back.

**Ta Bouche**

10-15 Market Passage, Cambridge CB2 3PF

Tel: +44 (0)1223 462277

www.tabouche.co.uk

Mon – Thurs: 10am-1am

Fri – Sat: 10am-2am

Sun: 10am-4pm, 9pm-12pm

*cocktails can be crafted to taste*

The year 2013 will see the 10th anniversary of this sophisticated bar. La Raza exudes all that is fabulous – food, drink and entertainment all encompassed under one roof. Set in the middle of the beautiful Rose Crescent, La Raza is in the very heart of the city.

Opening at noon on a daily basis, the bar slowly transforms throughout the day. Starting with lunch, there is a delicious Mediterranean menu consisting of tapas and salads, fish dishes and paellas. Complemented by a glass of wine from the well sourced list, what better way to spend a relaxed, comfortable time. Barista coffees are served all day which creates a smooth transition into the evening. The bar is open for delicious cocktails and aperitifs followed by dinner – food to share, hot and cold dishes and a great selection for vegetarians. Then, at 9pm, the bar goes through its final transition of the day as the music begins to play.

La Raza is known as a great venue for dancing. There are live bands every week with regulars such as Bijoumiyo and Swagger, guaranteed to get the crowd swinging. Wednesday nights are acoustic nights and, running alongside DJ events, jazz evenings and The Early Night club, there is always an event for everyone to have a marvellous time.

**La Raza**

4-6 Rose Crescent, Cambridge CB2 3LL
Tel: +44 (0)1223 464550
www.laraza.co.uk
Mon – Thurs: 11am-4pm, 7pm-1am
Fri – Sat: 11am-4pm, 7pm-2am

*great live music, djs... and cocktails!*

Picture the scene – you are on holiday and stumble across a bustling market square full of fruit and vegetables, flowers and flavoursome food items. On the corner of the market you notice an inviting terrace – full of tables and green umbrellas and people enjoying a morning coffee or a delicious-looking lunch. This image of the Mediterranean is kindly bought to you and the centre of Cambridge by the independent Italian restaurant Don Pasquale.

Established in 1973, Don Pasquale has been run by the same family ever since and enjoys a reputation for classic Italian cuisine, well-prepared and simply presented. With its Pizzeria and Gelateria, lovers of all things Italian can feel perfectly at home and children are well-catered for too with their own menu or half portions of all the main pasta dishes.

As well as breakfast, brunch and lunch, the atmospheric restaurant is also open in the evenings for dinner. The seven page menu offers pizzas, pasta, antipasto, salads, ciabattas and homemade desserts and if you need a recommendation, we suggest the Spaghetti alla Carbonara, the Penne con Pollo or one of the amazing Calzone Pizzas followed by the Affogato all' Amaretto. There is also a great selection of wines and Italian coffee.

Completing the authentic sense of a classic Italian restaurant is the open kitchen where you can watch a member of the family at work – always a positive sight in any restaurant.

**Don Pasquale**

12A Market Hill, Cambridge CB2 3NJ

Tel: +44 (0)1223 367063

Email: info@donpasquale.co.uk

www.donpasquale.co.uk

Mon – Sun: 8am-11pm

*come and meet Ed – probably the most well-known waiter in Cambridge!*

the UK's first outdoor market stall barber, and never appears to have a quiet moment since!

On Sundays (and bank holiday Mondays), the offering at the market changes when the stall holders for the Arts, Crafts and Local Produce Market lay out their wares. Introduced about 8 years ago, this market offers a quality selection of produce and products from the regions artists, craftspeople, photographers and farmers including unique gifts, jewellery, pottery, sculptures and organic foodstuff. It's also possible to pick up customised items as some of the stall holders can create these to your own design – so an opportunity to shop both independently as well as creatively.

Opposite the Guildhall is Cambridge's Market Square where around 100 stall holders set up each day to provide both visitors and locals with a colourful choice of goods and services.

Traditional market products such as fresh fruit, vegetables and flowers mix with Artisan bread, olives, health foods, fish, books, crafts, clothes, jewellery, antiques, records and CDs and is ever-changing as new stalls arrive. There are also a number of stalls offering services – it's possible to buy a handmade leather belt, get you bicycle fixed and get a haircut without leaving the Market Square – Francesco Scaglione chose Cambridge to set up as

### General and Sunday Markets

Market Square, Cambridge CB2
Tel: +44 (0)1223 457000
Email: info@love-cambridge.co.uk
www.cambridge.gov.uk/markets
General Market, Mon – Sat: 10am-4pm
Sunday Market, Sun: 10am-4pm
(and bank holiday Mons)

*granted its charter in 973 during the reign of Edgar the Peaceable*

## Cuckoo Owners: Kate and Michelle

Walking in to some clothing boutiques can be an intimidating experience – stern assistants, eye-watering price tags and overly clinical surroundings can halt you on the doorstep – but you need have no such fears at Cuckoo.

The genuinely bright and cheerful welcome from Kate , Michelle and the other members of the Cuckoo team is reflected in the layout of the shop too. White wooden floorboards and the use of reclaimed Victorian doors for the fittings gives a comforting, no-fuss feel, while showing of the range of clothes, accessories and gifts perfectly.

Originally inspired by the eclectic mix of items available in the markets and streets of Islington, Michelle and Kate have succeeded in bringing a fun, London style shopping experience to Cambridge. Always conscious of textiles, textures, patterns, cut and the real 'wearability' of clothing, Cuckoo chooses the designers it stocks on these criteria. Marilyn Moore, Odd Molly and Bombshell are amongst other lovingly-picked ranges, and collectively mix quirky designs with practical items to wear every day.

Complementing the clothes are gorgeous accessories including handbags, an ever-changing collection of jewellery, beautiful scarves in every texture and hue and girly gifts that are sure to please as presents for others or just for you!

### Cuckoo

4 St Mary's Passage
Cambridge CB2 3PQ
Tel: +44 (0)1223 364345
Email: info@cuckooclothing.co.uk
www.cuckooclothing.co.uk
Mon – Sat 9.30am-6.00pm
Sun – 11.00am-5.00pm

It is difficult to walk past Ark without being enticed in by the fabulous window display and then, the door opens onto an emporium of delightful treasures. This unique shop has the most eclectic selection of items where gifts can be found for interesting people.

Regular trips are made across Britain and Europe to source the best items – show stopping crystal creature jewellery, a massive spectrum of coloured leather Italian bags, and fabulous lamps that illuminate childhood memories. Long standing relationships with British companies see a constant supply of favourite items; wonderful leather gardening gloves from Shropshire and soothing, scented, paint-tin candles from Cumbria. There is also a great section dedicated to the very young; traditional and modern toys with a classic twist.

Always initiating new concepts, Jane has instigated a new delivery service. Using a local cycle courier company, perfect presents can be delivered to anywhere in Cambridge.

Jane's aim for Ark has always been to sell things that nobody else does – and that has certainly been achieved. From school bells, scorpions in paper weights, to chocolate lightbulbs, beetles in marbles and phrenology heads – there is always something intriguing to be found and something new waiting to be discovered.

**Ark**
2 St Mary's Passage
Cambridge CB2 3PQ
Tel: +44 (0)1223 363372
www.arkcambridge.co.uk
Mon – Sat: 9.30am-6pm
Sun: 10am-5pm

# G David Bookseller Owners: David, Brian and Neil

In 1896 the original G David (a Parisian bookseller) started selling his books from a stall in the central market square in Cambridge. Today, if you take a short walk from the market towards the Cambridge Arts Theatre and King's College, just next to St Edward's Church, you will find G David Bookseller in St Edward's Passage which surrounds the Church and has remained largely unchanged for centuries.

There could hardly be a more perfect location for a traditional book shop specialising in antiquarian books, fine bindings, second-hand books and publisher's remainders, so step inside G David Bookseller – fondly known by its customers simply as 'David's'.

Owned and run by the most welcoming team you could wish to meet, David's has that sense of being from another time – almost as if you have arrived at a location for a film where an archetypal English bookshop is required as a setting by the director.

Wind your way through the heavily-stocked rooms at the front of the shop and this 'film-set' sense is heightened when you walk into the antiquarian book room. Specialising particularly in English literature, early science and travel, the room contains about 4,000 beautifully bound books that surround you on shelves, in bookcases and on a large central table.

Hours could be spent here quite easily.

### G David Bookseller

16 St Edward's Passage, Cambridge CB2 3PJ
Tel: +44 (0)1223 354619
Email: g.david.books@gmail.com
www.gdavidbookseller.co.uk
Mon – Sat: 9am-5pm

Looking from the doorway, through the entrance of King's College, amazingly all the way to Queen's Road and the Backs beyond, you will experience the magic of Primavera's location. Turn around, and you are presented with the striking exterior of a beautiful listed building – once the home of the English essayist and poet Charles Lamb, and the base of the Society of Designer Craftsmen.

On Primavera's three ancient floors and corridors, you will discover 7,000 unique items of jewellery, ceramic, glass and silverware, as well as wonderful handmade scarves and ties, sculptures, glorious paintings and prints, cards and wrapping paper.

Famous jewellers and makers are juxtaposed against frequent arrivals of new work from upcoming artists and designers – many of whom live in Cambridgeshire – more than 400 British artists and designers in all!

The selection of jewellery is incredible – not only finely wrought gold, platinum and silver containing diamonds, emeralds, sapphires, rubies and all the semi-precious stones, but also aluminium, glass, resin and fabric. For the home and person, the range of ceramics and glassware is particularly special and for art lovers, the paintings and sculptures are different to what you will find anywhere else.

The ever changing displays and exhibitions, encapsulated in the tiny shop window opposite the entrance to King's, ensures that each return visit will yield new treasures. You can also be assured that your purchase is truly bespoke, always reasonably priced, sometimes expensive, but often very affordable, and you buy with the knowledge you are supporting not only Primavera and independent shops, but also the original artist and designer.

### Primavera

10 King's Parade, Cambridge CB2 1SJ
Tel: +44 (0)1223 357708
Email: contactprimavera@aol.com
www.primaverauk.com

*supporting British artists*

Seeing photographs of his grandfather on a mapping expedition to Tibet, a young Fin knew instantly that travel was in his blood too. Initially travelling to Afghanistan as a teenager and falling in love with the culture he found there, the question was how could he fund further journeys? The answer – to find and buy beautiful items and bring them back to Cambridge to sell, and so the seeds for Nomads were sown.

Fin continues to satisfy his wanderlust with annual trips, now mainly to India and Nepal, to discover new aspects of the cultures as well as sourcing interesting ranges for the shop. In fact all who work at Nomads love travel, which probably explains the friendly openness and enthusiasm of everyone there.

To discover for yourself what Fin has collected along the way, all you need to do is take a short walk downstairs at Nomads. The shop is on two floors but the lower floor really is a true Aladdin's Cave. Afghan rugs, scarves, shawls and stoles, clothing, throws, lampshades, wooden boxes, Tibetan singing bowls, tribal artifacts, stationary and musical instruments fill the room. And the range of jewellery is particularly impressive, the majority of it coming from Jaipur – the hub of the jewellery industry in Rajasthan.

Nomads also transforms into an atmospheric venue for evening talks and concerts – information for which can be found on the Nomads Facebook page along with stories and music from around the world.

### Nomads

5 Kings Parade, Cambridge CB2 1SJ
Tel: +44 (0)1223 324588
Email: nomadfin@gmail.com
www.nomads.uk.com
www.facebook.com/nomadskingsparade
Mon – Sat: 10am-6.30pm
Sun: 12am-5pm

the world awaits you downstairs at Nomads

# Cambridge Contemporary Crafts

Sister gallery to Cambridge Contemporary Art in Trinity Street, Cambridge Contemporary Crafts was opened in 2009 to showcase the ever expanding range of crafts.

Housed in a beautiful 16th century building located just opposite St Benet's Church, the oldest church in the City, and two doors down from the famous Eagle pub (where Francis Crick announced that he and James Watson had discovered the structure of DNA), the gallery is another attraction making this historic street a worthwhile destination for locals and visitors alike.

Showcasing crafts handmade in the UK, Cambridge Contemporary Crafts holds a huge range of work by up and coming as well as established craftspeople in the mediums of ceramics, glass, textiles, wood and jewellery. Throughout the year, the ever-changing display promotes the work of these artists and craftspeople – look out for, amongst others, the wonderfully organic finish of the ceramics by Carys Davies, the vintage patterns on the pieces by Katie Almond, the intricate and quirky sculptures by Shirley Vauvelle (using ceramics, driftwood, wire, reclaimed maps and other interesting materials) and beautiful jewellery by Henrietta Fernandez.

As, in the Trinity Street gallery, the atmosphere is friendly and genuinely helpful and prices start from just a few pounds. The Art Council's Own Art scheme is also available, making it easy and affordable to buy original, high-quality contemporary art and craft. You can borrow up to £2,000, or as little as £100, which is paid back interest free in equal instalments over a period of 10 months. The gallery also offers gift vouchers and runs a wedding list service.

More beautiful handmade work downstairs

**Cambridge Contemporary Crafts**
5 Bene't Street, Cambridge CB2 3QN
Tel: +44 (0)1223 361200
Email: info@cambridgecrafts.co.uk
www.cambridgecrafts.co.uk
Mon – Sat: 10am-5.30pm
Sun and Bank holidays: 11am-5pm

In 2011, Cambridge University alumnus Stephen Fry posted on Twitter that his favourite tea shop and bakery – Fitzbillies, was closing. Living in London at the time, but born and raised in Cambridge, Alison read the tweet and the idea to save a Cambridge institution was born.

So in August 2011 (after a lot of hard work), the 90 year-old story of Fitzbillies started a new chapter. The Grade II listed art deco frontage has been restored and the interior has a new and fresh look. Its famous Chelsea buns are as outrageously sticky as before (using the original recipe) and a very tasty cheese version is well worth a try. In addition to the buns and other tempting cakes and pastries, Fitzbillies has a lunch menu – including its 1938 Beef patties, savoury tarts and pies (from the bakery), soups, salads and terrines – and which changes daily to reflect seasonal availability.

Another new Fitzbillies storylines has been the addition of an exciting new dinner menu – currently available on Friday and Saturday nights but with hopefully more nights planned. The menu changes weekly (it's uploaded on the website usually on a Tuesday), and to give an idea of the style of food, dishes have included starters of backed figs with White Lady, walnut and honey and Fitzbillies mutton ham, spiced apricots, potted mutton on toasted potato rosemary bread. Main course offerings have seen delicious combinations such as aubergine charlotte, dandelion, croutons and mustard dressing and also braised rabbit with cos, bacon and new potatoes. And of course the deserts are pretty good too – well they would be!

### Fitzbillies

51-52 Trumpington Street, Cambridge CB2 1RG

Tel: +44 (0)1223 352500

Email: manager@fitzbillies.com

www.fitzbillies.com

*a new chapter for a Cambridge institution*

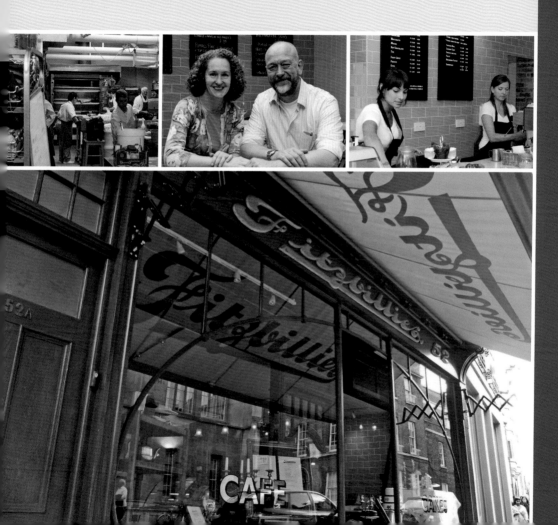

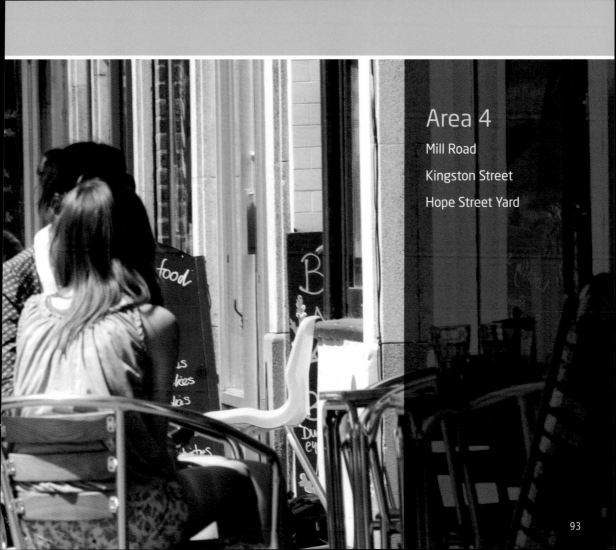

# Area 4

Mill Road

Kingston Street

Hope Street Yard

# Area 4

*Mill Road*

Mill Road used to be called Hinton Way (the way to Cherry Hinton). The road still ends in a footpath that leads to Cherry Hinton. Today's name comes from the Windmill that stood near the Salvation Army Shop (hence Mill Street too). The shop was previously Fine Fare, Cambridge's first supermarket! And before that it was The Playhouse Cinema.

Romsey Town was known as 'Little Russia' after the Master of a Cambridge College referred to the striking railwaymen who lived there as 'Bolsheviks' during the General Strike in 1926.

*Allan Brigham*

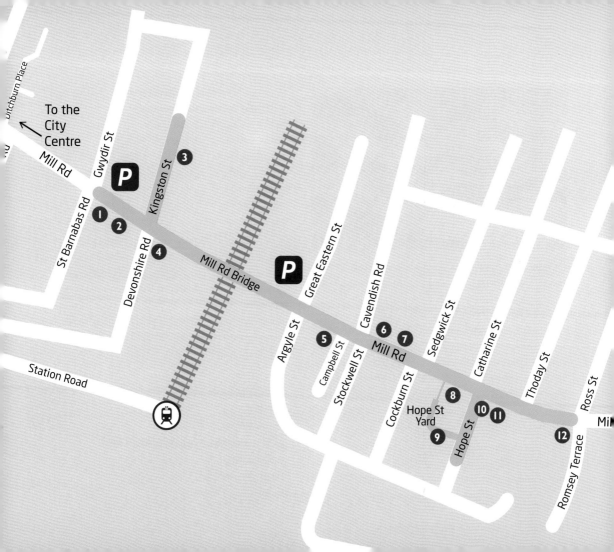

It's hard to believe looking around the stylish and modern interior at Taank Optometrists that an optician's practice has actually existed at 92A Mill Road for nearly 100 years, with Henry Flanders originally opening a combined Chemist, Dentist and Opticians at the site in 1913. Today, owner Anjana Taank, believes in combining some of those traditional values of customer service and community involvement with the most up-to-date eye health technology and eyewear fit for the seriously fashion conscious.

With her experience, of working not only in independent and multiple opticians but also in the hospital eye service and voluntarily abroad, Anjana is certainly someone you feel is passionate about what she does as well as incredibly knowledgeable in her chosen field. She continues to work closely with Cambridge's Addenbrooke's Hospital – in the Glaucoma Clinic within the Eye Department and provides clinical services for the hospital. This professional work has involved investing in the latest equipment as well as specialised training, so there is no doubt you are in safe, expert hands with Anjana.

And if you are (literally) on the lookout for top quality, fashionable frames and sunglasses, Anjana's range is hand-picked and selected to reflect style as well as quality. Both British and International designers are chosen for their unique, cutting-edge approach to design and manufacture, with the range including Booth and Bruce, Jono Hennesey, Markus T, William Morris London, Maui Jim and Porsche.

### Taank Optometrists

92A Mill Road, Cambridge CB1 2BD
Tel: +44 (0)1223 350071
Email: info@taankoptometrists.co.uk
www.taankoptometrists.co.uk
Mon – Sat: 9.00am-5.30pm

*worth a visit for the creative window displays alone!*

A classic case of looks can be deceiving. Al-Amin may look from the outside like an ordinary grocers, but once inside this deceptively large shop opens up to reveal a wealth of foods from around the world.

Many reviewers have described shopping at Al-Amin as 'an experience' – an often over-used phrase when it comes to shopping – but just so true in this case. The front of the shop contains a wonderfully exotic range of fresh produce – fruit, vegetables, herbs and spices all displaying county of origin (an education in itself). As well as traditional varieties, you can pick up guava, paw paw, granadilla, yams, okra, eddoe, matoke and apple bananas as well as fresh ginger and a wide selection of different types of chillies.

Explore further in to the store and discover foods from the Middle East, Africa, the Mediterranean, and Asia. The aptly named 'Spice and Rice Den' is a small room packed to the roof with every variety of rice and dried spice you could ever need for any recipe and if you fancy something more convenient, towards the back of the shop is the deli selling freshly made Indian and Thai dishes to takeaway. The website too contains a list of recipes so you can try out some dishes for yourself at home.

Also packed in to this wonderful store is a Halal butchers, a bakery and a post office which means there is a constant feeling of daily activity and also a sense that Al-Amin is definitely a very much-loved part of the local Mill Road community.

### Al-Amin

100A-102A Mill Road, Cambridge CB1 2BD

Tel: +44 (0)1223 576396

www.al-amin.com

Mon – Sat: 9am-7.30pm

Sun: 10am-7pm

*like a culinary expedition around the world*

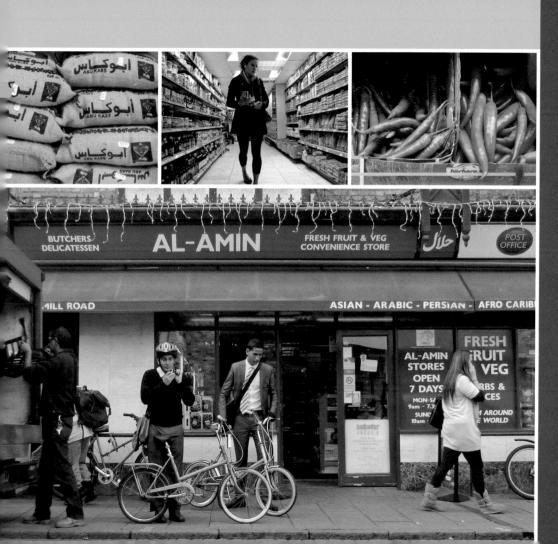

Richard – who was trained in the Hill tradition of bow making, and served a full apprenticeship with the legendary Garner Wilson – has gone on to develop his own style to include a wide range of influences. He produces baroque and classical, as well as modern bows and before becoming a bow maker, he was a professional viola player and teacher himself, and so is very sensitive to the needs of players.

In addition to making new bows, the repair, re-hair and restoration of old bows is undertaken with a same day service often available by arrangement, depending on the degree of work to be done.

If you happen to be enjoying a drink and something to eat in the Kingston Arms (a great independent pub off Mill Road), and you chance to look out of the window, you will no doubt notice the elegant hand-painted sign proclaiming the presence of a Bow Maker. In this mainly residential street of terraced houses, this is the only outward hint of the wonderful Aladdin's cave contained behind the workshop door of Richard Wilson – bow maker and repairer.

**Richard Wilson Bow Maker**
The Workshop, 36 Kingston Street
Cambridge CB1 2NU
Tel: +44 (0)1223 354115
Email: richardwilson.bowmaker@gmail.com
www.bowmaker.co.uk
Mon – Fri 9am-12.30pm and 2pm-5pm
or by appointment

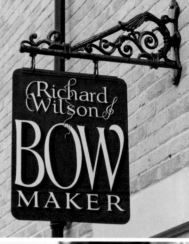

In 1999 the well-known Cambridge Butcher Mr Fabish handed over the keys to his shop in Mill Road to Andrew Northrop, and so began another chapter in the life of a butchers' shop that had existed on the same site since the early 1900s.

Andrew started in the trade immediately on leaving school at 16 – learning the business of being a butcher literally on-the-job. This experience taught him the importance of a good apprenticeship and he now has a rigorous training policy in place for all his staff.

The shop in Mill Road has flourished thanks to Andrew's commitment to selling only the best quality meat and offering a friendly and knowledgeable service to his customers and has allowed him to expand and open a second shop in Burleigh Street.

Inside both shops you will discover a carefully chosen selection of mainly locally-sourced meat including succulent Dingley Dell Pork from Suffolk and Label Anglais chickens from Essex. Temple Farm turkeys are also available at Christmas when you can see the queue from the shop snaking down Mill Road as people wait to collect their festive orders.

At Northrop's you can also pick up speciality items such as game, quails' eggs, Gurkha curry sauces, goose fat and different types of dripping. There's also a range of cured meats including Spanish chorizo, Boerewors (South African sausage) and Biltong – a variety of air-dried beef.

**Andrew Northrop Butchers**
114 Mill Road
Cambridge CB1 2BQ
Tel: +44 (0)1223 354779

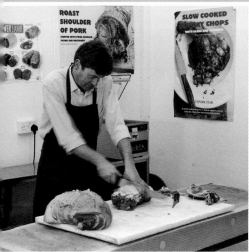

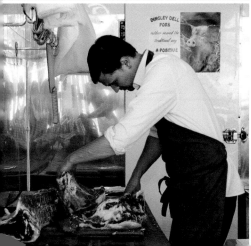

With such a large and continually growing community of artists in Cambridge, it's no surprise that a high-quality, bespoke picture framing service was established and continues to flourish in Mill Road.

Moving to the city in 1985, John, with his artistic background, explored the art scene and saw a need for a good-value, bespoke framing service. So, in 1989, Frameworks was founded. From an original leaflet drop in the local area it steadily built its customer base of artists to include local people, businesses, organisations and photographers and by 2002 the workshop had doubled in size.

As a member of The Fine Art Trade Guild and with 23 years experience, there are not many framing jobs that Frameworks cannot handle. The workshop frames all sorts of artworks, certificates, sports shirts, medals, memorabilia and artefacts that people pick up on their travels. With a huge choice of frame styles and mountboard colours to choose from, Frameworks is able to offer a service which truly enhances and complements the varied items being framed. Plain wood frames are popular and can also be hand-finished with stains and waxes.

For those more precious pictures that need to be conserved for future generations, Frameworks offers a full Conservation Framing Service using archival, acid-free materials and ultra-violet shielding glass which greatly reduces any 'sunlight-fade' that might occur over many years.

In 2011, continued growth enabled John to open a shop (with parking) on Mill Road, just across from the workshop. Now, with four staff as well as John, it looks as if the need for good-quality, reasonably-priced bespoke framing is still growing.

**Frameworks**
170 Mill Road, Cambridge CB1 3LP
Tel: +44 (0)1223 213092/778817
Email: info@frameworks-cambridge.co.uk
www.frameworks-cambridge.co.uk
Mon, Tues, Wed, Fri: 10am-6pm  Sat: 11am-4pm
Closed for lunch: 1pm-1.30pm except for Sat
Closed Thurs and Sun and Bank holidays

SEE OUR WEBSITE FOR LATEST OFFER

Urban Larder has been on the Broadway in Mill Road for nearly two years, having outgrown its original home in Hope Street Yard. It's fast-gaining popularity for good, locally-sourced food is not surprising with many delights such as local honey, jams from the Country Markets, bacon, ham, venison, cheeses from The Wobbly Bottom Farm, healthy ready meals, Saffron Ice Creams, pickles, mustards, local farm eggs – both duck and hen and 100 percent organic baked bread – kneaded by local people, with heart and soul in every loaf!

Polly is also gaining a reputation for stocking some of the widest range of gluten- and wheat-free food as well as vegetarian and vegan treats. Alongside all the yummy food, is a display of work by local artists and lovely wrapping papers, gifts and cards.

With its pretty and quirky seating area, you can 'try before you buy', as all of the sandwich fillings, quiches and salads can be bought in the shop. A very popular addition to the lunchtime menu is the superb Greek slice. Made from 'his mother's own recipe', Yannis (from Crete), brings Polly both a spinach and goat's cheese feta slice in olive oil pastry and a potato, courgette and herb alternative.

And with evening events such as the ever-popular Pavitt's Pie and Mash night and its general place as a 'hub' for many of the locals, the Urban Larder provides the community with so much more than just its great selection of free-range, homemade and sustainable food choices.

### Urban Larder

9, The Broadway, Mill Road
Cambridge, CB1 3NA

Tel: +44 (0)1223 212462

Email: info@urbanlarder.co.uk

www.urbanlarder.co.uk

Mon: 12pm-5pm

Tues – Weds: 10am-6pm

Thurs: 10am-9pm (Soup Night)

Fri: 10am-9/9.30pm (Vinyl Nights)

Sat: 10am-6pm

Sun: 11am-5pm

**SPECIAL OFFER**

10% off
eat-in
lunch bill

*Polly's favourite - Country market's biscuits*

WET FISH £/kg

| | | |
|---|---|---|
| COD | NORTH EAST ATLANTIC | 9.50 |
| HADDOCK | FRESH / GRIMSBY SMOKED | 9.50 / 13.50 |
| LUXURY FISH PIE MIX | | 14.50 |
| | SALMON, COD, MONKFISH, SM. HADDOCK, PRAWNS | |
| SALMON | SCOTTISH | 14.20 |
| PLAICE | | 16.50 |
| SHETLAND MUSSELS (ROPE GROWN) | | 6.50 |
| SEA BASS & BREAM | WHOLE | 9.80 / 8.20 |
| SQUID | | 12.50 |
| | SQUID INK 80p PER SACHET | |
| TROUT | WHOLE ENGLISH RAINBOW | 10.50 |

Mill Road's alternative fish bar, (finalist in the BBC Radio 4 2011 Food and Farming Awards and Highly Commended in the Best Newcomer category at the UK National Fish & Chip Awards), certainly offers the fish lovers out there a large number of alternative ways to get their fish fix. A traditional take-away fish and chip shop The Sea Tree has a number of stylishly simple wooden tables for dining in-house, and a wet fish section.

Fresh fish deliveries arrive from Grimsby or direct from Billingsgate Market. David also insists that their suppliers provide written guarantee the fish is from traceable and sustainable well-managed sources.

Fish is prepared – deep fried, grilled or pan fried – all cooked to order. You can also have your batter gluten-free. Alongside traditional fish such as cod, haddock and plaice, the regular menu carries delicious alternatives including fish stew, calamari, salmon, trout, bream, sea bass and fisherman's pie. Along with other seasonal treats on offer like grilled Cornish Sardines, Scallops and Shetland Mussels. And just to add that little extra uniqueness, to accompany your fish is a range of homemade sauces.

As if that's not enough choice you can visit The Sea Tree for Sunday Brunch from 10am till 2pm where Grilled Kippers, Eggs Benedict, Kedgeree and Eggs Florentine are amongst the featured dishes.

### The Sea Tree

13/14, The Broadway, Mill Road
Cambridge CB1 3AH
Tel: +44 (0)1223 414349
www.theseatree.co.uk
Mon – 5-10pm
Tues, Wed, Thurs. 12-2pm, 5-10pm
Fri: 12 noon-2.30pm, 5-10pm
Sat: 12 noon-10pm
Sun: 10am-2pm (April – October), 5pm-9pm

*His favourite fish dish - pan-fried scallops!*

Voted one of the top 10 Italian delis in the UK in the 2012 Bertolli Olive D'Oro Awards, Limoncello disproves the belief that all the best Italian food in the UK is only found in London.

Not that the regulars (and there are many) are in any doubt. With some ninety percent of the shop's stock being imported directly from Italy and hand-picked by Steve on his frequent trips to the country, the range of fresh and other foodstuffs is constantly being added to with newly discovered delights. Particular regular favourites are the four varieties of fresh pesto – the rocket pesto is wonderful – and there is an equally tempting range of olives, antipasti, cheeses, sausages, meats, biscuits and pastries. Luring you in even further with its enticing aroma is the major line of non-Italian produce that Limoncello stocks in the form of freshly-baked bread. Steve takes daily deliveries from two local Italian bakeries, giving customers the choice between 'Cambridge' and 'Peterborough' bread. He also bakes a range of baguettes and ciabatta on-site which are then used for the handmade-to-order sandwiches, which can contain pretty much any combination of the fresh deli items in the shop.

A fairly recent addition to the shop is a small seating area and counter with stools for customers to enjoy something to eat and drink 'in-store'. It's not surprising that with such nice surroundings and tempting treats, with Steve and the rest of the team always happy to chat, that this has rapidly become a popular place for locals and visitors to congregate.

**Limoncello**
212 Mill Road, Cambridge CB1 3NF
Tel: +44 (0)1223 507036
www.limoncello.co.uk
Mon – Sat: 9am-9pm
Sun: 10am-5pm

**SPECIAL OFFER**

**Free espresso when you spend over £15**

*from his first try of panettone, Steve was hooked on the tastes of Italy!*

Cambridge Bread

Large Bread
£2.50

Just off Mill Road is Hope Street Yard – a community in its own right with second-hand and collectible sellers, a picture framer, a tailor, a musical instrument maker, a psychic, an electric bike company, plus, The School Run Centre, also known as Cambridge Dutch Bikes.

The popularity of this style of bike is evident on the streets of Cambridge. You will be hard pressed to find a teenage girl (in particular), who is not peddling around on a Dutch bike with the ubiquitous wicker basket on the front. Also popular amongst young families are the wonderful child carrying bikes and tricycles stocked by Hugh in his School Run Centre. The different permutations on how to transport varying numbers of small children as well as the weekly shopping (and your pet dog) appear endless but all catered for. And as the Yard is traffic free, you can test drive a Cargobike, mummybike, tandem or tricycle in safety.

As well as being kitted out for your 'wheels', you can satisfy your accessory cravings too. Baskets, matching panniers and child seats are all available to complete the look.

All of the bikes are imported directly from Holland, with brands including Azor, Bakfiets.nl Cargobike, Bakfiets.nl Cargotrike, BSP and Onderwater.

**The School Run Centre**
Hope Street Yard, Mill Road
Cambridge CB1 3NA
Tel: +44 (0)7772 738899
www.schoolruncentre.co.uk
Weds – Sat 12-6pm

As with a lot of studios and workshops, you would never guess from the outside, the extraordinary creativity and craftsmanship to be found just off a busy, urban high street – the sign outside only giving a small hint of what amazing things are happening behind the door.

Jonathan Woolston – maker and restorer of violins, violas and cellos and the man behind the hand-painted sign for Woolston Violins – is very much at home in the creative and independent area of the City that is Mill Road.

After studying at the Newark School of Violin Making, his experience accumulated through his work in various ateliers – most notably the Manhattan workshop of the renowned Jacques Français, where he learnt expertise and restoration techniques studying under one of the world's most respected violin makers and restorers – René Morel (1932-2011). Working in such a highly-regarded environment has bought Jonathan in to contact with such luminaries of the music world as Issac Stern, Pinchas Zukerman, Itzak Perlman, Yo-Yo Ma, Steven Isserlis, Tasmin Little & Maxim Vengerov to name just a handful.

Today, Jonathan looks after the magnificent collection of bowed string instruments at the Royal Academy of Music in London and also has worked on various projects with Cambridge University. In the last 10 years Jonathan has made about 40 instruments, both for local amateur musicians and for professional players. There are always new instruments available in the workshop to try out.

And just to think, all this knowledge and expertise is just a stone's throw from the local Co-op!

**Woolston Violins**
222 Mill Road, Cambridge CB1 3NF
Tel: +44 (0)1223 413860
Email: jwwoolston@gmail.com
www.woolstonviolins.com

Sometimes translation from one language to another, particularly if it's a cultural reference, can be difficult. Owner of Eastwind, Liliana, describes her shop as containing 'dreams'. This sounds strange until she tells you the story of a customer for whom she made 900 large, white, origami Japanese paper cranes for her wedding day. The customer had wanted white lanterns but was told these would traditionally have been exclusively used at funerals and not for weddings, so the birds were suggested and painstakingly created instead.

This story sums up Eastwind. Not only is it a place where you can find unique and often handmade items, but also a place where you can discover the real culture of the Orients and receive incredible service too.

Eastwind started in 2001 selling mainly large, antique pieces of furniture and other items imported from China as well as from all over Asia.

The shop still stocks incredible pieces of furniture, the majority of which are sold to customers further afield. However, for Cambridge customers, Liliana decided to stock a range of other items, which would be more practical, so, as well as large and small furniture, ceramics, bronze, carvings and ornaments, Eastwind sells the most beautiful collection of Chinese boxes, teapots, dolls, jade jewellery, games and instruments, calligraphy and painting sets and handmade cards.

With some of these lovely things costing from as little as 50 pence, you just really need to walk over the bridge on Mill Road and see what gift ideas Eastwind has in store for you.

**Eastwind Ltd, Cambridge**

224 Mill Road, Cambridge CB1 3NS

Tel: +44 (0)1223 471262

Mon – Fri: 11am-6pm

Sat: 10am-7pm

Sun: 1pm-5pm

*just walk over the bridge to discover real Chinese culture*

Situated on the Romsey side of Mill Road bridge, Cutlacks is not only the archetypal aladdin's cave of all things for the home and garden but is also, thanks to Steve, very much at the heart of the local community. There wouldn't be a Romsey Garden Club if it wasn't for Steve!

Cutlacks has been trading (from its other shop in Ely) for over 160 years and that sense of traditional customer service and help from your local hardware store is still very much part of the current shopping experience. DIY advice is readily offered on the large range of products in that department as well as in all the others – kitchen, home and gardens, bedroom, bathroom and linen, cutlery, glass and china and curtains.

Alongside traditional products for the home and garden you can find many contemporary brands including Joseph Joseph, Nigela Lawson, Hairy Bikers, Farrow and Ball, Fired Earth, Little Greene, Simply Human, Brabantia and many others that all go to make Cutlacks infinitely practical and also a pleasure to the eyes of some of its more design-conscious clientele.

A constant stream of shoppers visit Cutlacks – by foot, by bike, by bus (there is a stop just near the shop) but for those planning to buy larger items there is a car park, alternatively, purchases can be delivered – all part of the service.

### Cutlacks

264-268 Mill Road, Cambridge CB1 3NF
Tel: +44 (0)1223 246418
www.cutlacks.co.uk
Mon – Sat: 9am-5.30pm

More To Discover

MARVELOUS SCRAP PAPER

# More To Discover

Right across Cambridge, from the banks of the Cam in Chesterton to the North, to the City boundary near Grantchester in the South, we have discovered wonderful independents offering incredible variety.

As well as shopping independently for the best wine, freshly-made artisan bread and speciality foods, we have discovered artists, craftspeople, creative courses and galleries alongside restaurants and cafés serving delicious food you will not find anywhere else.

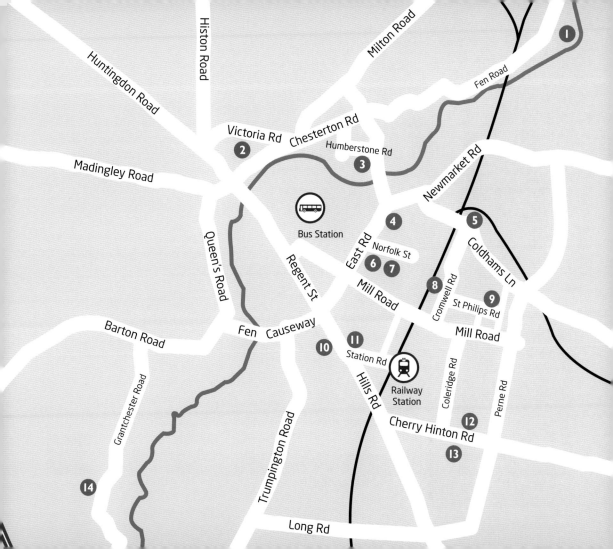

# White House Arts Director: Caroline Amory

Cambridge is the sort of place that however well you think you know it, there always seems to be something interesting and new to discover. This is how it feels on first finding out about White House Arts.

Idyllically located in the Chesterton area of the City on the banks of the Cam, White House Arts offers arts and crafts courses at its independent arts centre.

Complementing perfectly this beautiful setting is the ethos of creating a social and therapeutic atmosphere in which people can gain expertise and be creatively inspired.

Courses are run during the day, weekends and evenings and cover a wide range of creative disciplines including ceramics, textiles, mixed media, creative drawing, jewellery, kiln and stained glass, print making and sculpture, to name just a selection from the recent programme. White House Arts is a registered charity and all the courses are designed for those age 18 years and over.

All the tutors are artists in their own right with a professional approach to tutoring which, together with small class sizes, ensures all the students gain excellent experience and achieve a sense of accomplishment and satisfaction on completing their finished pieces.

Some students become so accomplished that they showcase at Open Studios and exhibitions.

With a significant number of students returning term after term, professionalism combined with a friendly and welcoming approach appear to be the perfect combination.

**White House Arts**

72 Fen Road, Cambridge CB4 1UN

Tel: +44 (0)1223 420018

Email: info@whitehousearts.co.uk

www.whitehousearts.co.uk

## Bacchanalia Owner: Paul Bowes

Bacchanalia (the business, not the debauched Roman festival!), was established on Victoria Road in 1997. Taking over the Jug & Firkin in Mill Road in 1999, it became, not so much a chain, but more of a link across Cambridge. Since then, with the philosophy of enjoying themselves and being nice to their customers, things have gone rather well.

The Victoria Road shop is your classic wine merchant, with a huge selection of wonderful wines, and also some of the best beers and spirits known to man. Paul, the owner, is nearly always behind the desk, ready to recommend wines and engage in any banter.

The Mill Road shop is considered their 'rough diamond'. It stocks a fine selection of beer, superb wines and a hugely eclectic spirit selection. The shop even has draught beer, poured straight from the tap – take away your container of lovely frothy beer, have a great night, then bring it back when you fancy a refill. No waste, no recycling, just smiles all round. Ed is the man at the Mill Road shop, cricket lover and all rounder – more in the drinking sense than the cricket sense.

The third member of staff is Jim, who covers both shops and writes on beer. He is an absolute fountain of knowledge, with a true passion for all things hedonistic!

Bacchanalia hold regular tastings sessions at both shops. If you would like to hear about tastings and other events you can join their mailing list to find out just what's coming up and when.

### Bacchanalia
79 Victoria Rd, Cambridge CB4 3BS
Tel: +44 (0)1223 576292
90 Mill Road, Cambridge CB1 2BS
Tel: +44 (0)1223 315034
www.winegod.co.uk

World Beers / Lagers

Bacchanalia
the Wine & spirits experts

Bacchanalia
Wine Merchants

To do is to be-Rousseau
To be is to do-Sartre
Dobedobedo-Sinatra

# Rowan

Not far from the Cam where it passes Midsummer Common, and situated in the predominantly residential Humberstone Road, is Rowan – a charity and arts centre, set up in 1985, which brings artists and people with learning difficulties together to create the most incredible items of fine artwork and craft.

Many of the pieces made by the students are on display in the gallery and are for sale including beautiful paintings, ceramics, sculptures and carved wooden items such as mirrors – the proceeds from which provide essential income for Rowan, allowing them to continue providing such collaborative opportunities for creativity and self-expression. The quality of the work is so good that the students at Rowan are also commissioned to work on specific pieces and projects, giving them a great sense of self-worth and self-esteem as well as developing their creative skills.

As many of the staff are practicing artists in their own right, it's not surprising that the work produced is of such a high standard. But it goes beyond creativity, as each person is nurtured to help them reach their full personal potential. A visit to Rowan brings this sense of empowerment very much to the forefront, particularly if you are able to see the students at work in one of the four studios.

Rowan is always welcoming to visitors, just get in touch first to make sure someone is there. They also hold regular open events and are part of Cambridge's annual Open Studios – details are on the website or join the mailing list to receive news on what's coming up.

**Rowan**
40 Humberstone Road, Cambridge CB4 1JG
Tel: +44 (0)1223 566027
Email: info@rowanhumberstone.co.uk
www.rowanhumberstone.co.uk

*Creating art, improving lives*

Since 1945 the objective of Primavera has been to create a stunning showcase for British contemporary art and design, by helping artists and makers with finance, origination and exhibition space. Since 1999 Jeremy Waller has continued this legacy.

Living through the conflict in Beirut in the early 1980s, and while travelling extensively through the Lebanon and Syria, Jeremy witnessed the stark contrast of awful civil conflict like the massacres at Sabra and Shatila, often involving him personally, with the beauty and history of its people and the wealth of architecture and landscape. On his return from there, and living for many years in Paris France and Nairobi Kenya, where he was born, Jeremy finds Primavera a way to make a difference in the world by helping and promoting artists, and inspiring visitors through displays of the most extraordinary, relevant and exciting artwork.

Open by appointment only, the gallery at Wellington Court is the most recent addition to the Primavera family. This modern space is the backdrop for a diverse collection of contemporary innovations in British art and design in a spacious atmosphere (purposefully different to King's Parade) to bring out the best in the individual pieces.

Currently Wellington Court is showing breathtaking glass by Peter Newsome, beautifully handcrafted wooden furniture by Peter Mundell, and luminous paintings by Robert Latoś.

The Wellington Court Gallery is a chance to experience contemporary British art and design in a new way; call now to begin your own journey.

**Primavera**
6 Wellington Court, Cambridge CB1 1HZ
Tel: +44 (0)1223 357708
Email: contactprimavera@aol.com
www.primaverauk.com

*Contemporary British art and design*

# St Barnabas Press Owner: James Hill

Originally located in St Barnabas Road (hence the name), St Barnabas Press is a fantastic open access, fine art printmaking studio, creative venue and gallery. Its current home just off Coldhams Lane near the common may look anonymous enough, but step inside to find magnificent old presses in a workshop buzzing with activity.

St Barnabas Press contains 14 individual studios which are rented to local artists, designers, creatives and craftspeople. It also provides open access membership and hot-desk space to those who want to use the facilities on a more flexible basis. Over the past 20 years, the press has become an amazing communal environment, where resident artists, open access members and visitors alike can meet to collaborate and share ideas.

There is a perennial programme of printmaking and arts education. Courses in etching, wood-cut, screen and relief printing are complemented by opportunities to learn animation and photography, as well as foundation skills like life drawing.

The press is owned and run by master printer, James Hill. Artists and designers wishing to produce print editions can collaborate with James, to ensure their work is produced to the highest standards available. In addition to the more traditional methods of printmaking, there are two large format digital printers and scanning and photographic facilities to provide a cutting-edge imaging and reproduction service.

St Barnabas Gallery exhibits a rolling programme of new works for sale by resident and visiting artists from all over the globe. Smaller items include wonderful handmade cards and sketch books made from cotton paper with individual covers made by the printmakers – making each one, completely unique.

**St Barnabas Press**
Coldhams Road, Cambridge CB1 3EW
Tel: +44 (0)1223 413792
www.stbarnabaspress.co.uk
stbarnabaspress.webplus.net

Walking down Norfolk Street, there is no better place to stop for a break than the delightful Box Café. Set back from the road enables a pleasant outside seating area and inside it is light and airy. Good size tables ensure plenty of room for friends and family.

Opening good and early at 8am, it is a great way to start the day with Ozy's cheery, welcoming smile and a hearty breakfast. As the morning moves through to lunchtime, the international menu comes into its own. Italian pasta dishes and French baguettes are made to order, or there is the most delicious selection of meze. Whether vegetarian or meat

based, it is all freshly prepared on a daily basis. Served with warm pittas it is the most enjoyable of lunches.

The afternoon is a fine excuse for a treat. Sit and relax with a fine cup of coffee or tea and a scrumptious piece of home-made cake – what could be better after a busy day.

There is also a function room available at the Box – a great venue for a party with a Turkish feast, or to hire out to run classes such as yoga or dance. Ozy has recently introduced popular live music evenings and craft events, making this the most versatile of venues.

**The Box Café**
47 Norfolk Street
Cambridge CB1 2LD
Tel: +44 (0)1223 576110
www.theboxcafe.co.uk
Mon – Sat: 8am-6pm

# Adilia's Norfolk Street Bakery Owner: Adilia Frazao

There has been a bakery at 89 Norfolk Street since 1868, and this year saw its doors open again with a fresh new look and a keen young baker – Adilia.

It's a pretty early start for anyone who is in the business of running a bakery. So considering Adilia's day sees her up and baking at 3am, it's a good thing she is so passionate about bread. Fond childhood memories of taking over in the kitchen of her home in Portugal when her mother was out, coupled with discovering her love of bread and pastry while working as a chef in London, Adilia has the knowledge as well as the passion for what she does.

The artisan breads are made using organic flour and include British classics such as sourdough, wholemeal and bloomers, as well as tempting Mediterranean rustic bread and rolls and the very popular rich German Ryes. Each week, Adilia introduces something new for her customers like focaccia or the very moreish chorizo rolls and like all the breads, are baked on-site every day.

And for the sweet-toothed, there is the chance to try out various Portuguese-influenced cakes and pastries. Along with muffins, Danish pastries and brownies, Adelia makes Portuguese custard tarts and other cakes inspired by her homeland. She has learnt that not all are to the taste of some of her British customers, but she relishes the creative challenge of tailoring the ingredients and trying out her new ideas.

**Adilia's Norfolk Street Bakery**

89 Norfolk Street, Cambridge CB1 2LD

Tel: +44 (0)1223 660163

www.facebook.com/pages/Adilias-Norfolk-Street-Bakery/111934352293578

Mon – Fri: 7.30am-5.30pm

Sat: 8.30am-2.00pm

*A meal is not a meal without bread*

Just off Mill Road, on the Romsey side of the bridge and at the end of either Sedgwick Street or Catharine Street, is a relatively new addition to the growing contemporary and visual art scene in the City – the Cambridge Art Salon.

Celebrating its first birthday in September 2012, the Salon is a real community venture, offering work space and gallery space to members of the public from the Cambridge area. Working as an artist can be very isolating, but at the Salon there is the chance for people to meet, support each other and also collaborate in a nurturing and affordable environment.

And of course there is the opportunity to purchase some of the work – what better way to support independent artists? Cambridge Art Salon has, on-site, a range of artists and creative practitioners working in contemporary arts and creative media. They are able to use the gallery space to showcase the diverse and vibrant work they produce, across an exciting range of disciplines. Exhibitions are obviously regular events on the calendar and so are art classes for both adults and children.

Realising too the increasing number of other exciting contemporary art spaces throughout the City, Cambridge Art Salon has created 'The Cambridge Art Walks Map'. Featuring galleries in the City centre as well as those further off the beaten track, the map shows just how much exciting work is happening and waiting to be discovered.

**Cambridge Art Salon**

29 Cromwell Road
Cambridge CB1 3EB
Tel: +44 (0)1223 244391
Email: info@cambridgeartsalon.org.uk
www.cambridgeartsalon.org.uk
Thurs: 5.30pm-7pm  Fri: 10am-5.30pm
Fri evenings: private views & opening parties
Sat – Sun: 10am-5.30pm

*Featured artist (bottom right photo) Sadie Few*

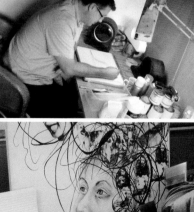

Once again, the streets of Cambridge prove to harbour a wealth of artistic talent and creativity. Along with fine musical instrument makers, painters, printmakers, ceramicists and photographers, Harry Gray creates work on an altogether different scale.

Having specialised in Public Art at art school, Harry knew the importance of acquiring the necessary skills required to produce work of the highest possible standard and so moved to Cambridge to train as a stone carver. The training gave him the confidence to take on some major public work such as the Battle of Britain Monument at Dover, a joint project with Landscape Architect Jamie Buchanan, which ignited an interest in war and how it is commemorated. His approach to this brief was a more contemplative rather than combative look at warfare, but he also believes its right to sometimes take a critical and more reflective stance, particularly towards heavily controversial conflicts.

On a more local level, one of Harry's Cambridge-based projects was creating a row of stacks of bronze books outside the Cambridge University Library. A challenging commission with such a powerful architectural backdrop, but with an open brief and a supportive client, the result with its interactive swivelling towers of books, has proved a popular attraction.

The other strand to Harry's work has a strong figurative element and he makes sure he finds time every week to draw as it is fundamental to everything he does. A recent creative interest has seen him casting figurative elements from historic buildings to make new sculpture for exhibition. This type of non-commissioned sculpture is something Harry is keen to do more of in the future.

**Harry Gray Sculptor**
The Studio, 53A St. Philips Road
Cambridge CB1 3DA
Tel: +44 (0)1223 410751
www.harrygray.co.uk

*a constantly changing body of work*

# Le Gros Franck and Alliance Française de Cambridge

Being famous for its university means Cambridge is home to people from all over the world. Some stay for a short time while others make it their home. Bringing a true flavour of France to the City are restaurant Le Gros Franck and French cultural centre, L'Alliance Française de Cambridge – both located close to each other on Hills Road, near to the station.

By day, Le Gros Franck, the only truly independent French restaurant in Cambridge, is a bustling and atmospheric Café/Patisserie, offering fresh Pastries, Crepes, Quiches and filled Baguettes accompanied by the most amazing salad bar. Traditional hot dishes include genuine French-style Bœuf Bourguignon and Steak-Frites and there is always a 'Fish of the day' and tempting vegetarian options available – all to either enjoy eating in or to take away. By night, award-winning chef Franck Parnin creates regional French dishes cooked just as they should be, such as filet de Boeuf Rossini, Confit de Canard and Escargot Persilles.

Complementing this gastronomic, cultural experience are the varied activities offered by l'Alliance Française de Cambridge, the oldest cultural organisation of its kind in the world. Along with taylor made French courses and drop-in conversation sessions (some of which are free and held at Le Gros Franck), the organisation holds regular events including concerts, talks, festival celebrations, visits to museums and children's workshops. All are open to French and non-French speakers and are a really enjoyable way of learning the language and discovering French culture.

### Le Gros Franck

57 Hills Road, Cambridge CB2 1NT
Tel: +44 (0)1223 565560
www.legrosfranck.com
Mon – Wed: 7am-5.30pm  Thurs – Sat: 7am-5.30pm
Evening dinner 6.15pm-9.30pm
Sun: 8am-4.30pm

### Alliance Francaise de Cambridge

60 Hills Road, Cambridge CB2 1AL
Tel: +44 (0)1223 561854
www.alliance-cam.co.uk

# Linford Joinery Owner: James Linford

The youngest and newest of our featured independents – James was setting up Linford Joinery literally as this first edition of Independent Cambridge went to press.

Although at the beginning of the independent road, James is a fully-qualified, time-served bench joiner with a background in the construction and installation of doors, windows and staircases.

The new enterprise is all of the above plus customised, hand-crafted furnishings and fittings for domestic and commercial environments.

Offering a bespoke service, James will build and install elegant replacement sash windows to meet modern building regulations; craft doors from selected softwood or hardwood; design and fit a unique staircase or create a tailored piece of stylish fitted furniture to sit perfectly in the room it was made for. Mouldings, too, can be made to accommodate the different quirks, dimensions and angles of any room – particularly those of period properties and they can also be recreated to match existing moulding details.

From the initial choice of wood used, through to the different finishes available, James uses his experience and expertise to offer advice as to the best options depending on the job in-hand. He also understands the potential restrictions surrounding planning regulations and listed building status and so ensures all of his work is carefully designed, not only to the highest standards of craftsmanship but also to work perfectly and practically in-situ.

**Linford Joinery**
217B Cherry Hinton Road
Cambridge CB1 7DA
Tel: +44 (0)7449 834098
Email: linfordjoinery@gmail.com
https://www.facebook.com/
Linfordjoinerycambridge?fref=ts

For more than 40 years, the Balzano family has been supplying Cambridge with the finest Italian delicacies, handmade daily from original family recipes brought from Puglia, Italy.

Their bakery, which is housed inside the Cherry Hinton Road delicatessen and café, begins turning out bread every morning at 4am, providing the shop and its loyal customers around Cambridge with the freshest loaves, pastries and cakes.

Balzano's deli offers an incredible range of cheeses, meats, olives and other fresh, Italian foods as well as locally produced Pavitt's Pies. On the shelves are stacked preserves, oils, wine, coffee and roughly 100 different types of pasta (Becky has stopped counting). If you dare, peep in the freezer and be

tempted by a wide selection of ice creams. Most items come from Italian wholesalers, and some are exclusively produced in Italy for Balzano's.

In 2011, the shop underwent a complete refit and unveiled a stylish retro-designed café that has inspired a new generation of customers – home and office workers, mums and children among them – who in the mornings gather in the attractive eatery to nibble pain au chocolat, sip Italian coffees, and enjoy a sense of community. A robust lunchtime menu includes gourmet sandwiches filled with Italian specialities and aromatic pan-baked pizza.

For a particularly Italian experience, head to the shop at Christmas time when boxes of Panettone are displayed from every spare hook, shelf and counter. With more than 4,000 of the traditional sweet bread loaves ordered every year, the colourful packages adorn the shop like decorations, and the holidays beckon.

### Balzano's Delicatessen

204 Cherry Hinton Road, Cambridge CB1 7AW

Tel: +44 (0)1223 246168

Email: balzanosdeli@gmail.com

Mon – Fri: 8.30am-5.30pm

Sat: 8am-4pm

## The Blue Ball Owners: John and Karolin

Probably the best way to describe The Blue Ball is to begin by listing the things it doesn't have. To start with, it doesn't have any lager or a long row of pumps proclaiming a myriad of different beer names on the bar. It also doesn't have an extensive dining menu – in fact there is no menu at all. There is no television, no juke box and certainly no karaoke machine, in other words, no distractions. As one regular (and there are many) once said, "ninety-nine percent of people just don't get it, but the one percent who do – love it!"

What The Blue Ball does have is lots of banter, conversation around an open fire, a picturesque view across to Grantchester Meadows, the wonderfully named 'smokatorium' in the garden filled with pictures of cricket matches, books and blankets for when it gets cold, and above all – it has top quality beer.

John has been in the trade all his life and when Greene King sold the pub on, John immediately bought in Adnams as his regular, 'quaffing' beer. In addition there is a different beer each week such as Bass, London Pride or Landlord and with only two pumps, this ensures the beer is the best it can be. As John points out, "beer is only good if you are selling it".

It's easy to walk, cycle or even punt to The Blue Ball and if you happen to be a dog owner – you will find a very warm welcome indeed!

**The Blue Ball**
57 Broadway, Grantchester
Cambridge CB3 9NQ
Tel: +44 (0)1223 840679
Mon – Fri: 2pm-11pm
Sat and bank holidays: 12pm-12am
Sun: 12pm-10pm

# Indies On The Web

# The Biscuit Jar Owner: Rachel Hewlett

All of us have special occasions to celebrate – births, birthdays, anniversaries, starting a new job, Christmas – the list is endless. However, finding a unique gift to celebrate and mark these events can sometimes be difficult.

Step in Rachel Hewlett and her new company – The Biscuit Jar. Having previously worked in the food services industry, including as a buyer for Selfridges, the arrival of her sons prompted a look at her work/life balance. The gift of a cookie cutter, mixed with an entrepreneurial spirit and passionate foodie Rachel was inspired to develop her own range of handcrafted, decorated biscuits.

The sweet varieties use intricate icing to make delicious, edible works of art and can be custom designed to suit pretty much any occasion. A recent jar of biscuits Rachel created was to mark a 50th wedding anniversary, with each of the sweet treats representing something from their many years together.

A savoury range is also available including pre dinner aperitif parmesan and fennel biscuits and a rye, poppy seed and oat biscuit selection, great to serve with cheese. For added fun, these can be cut into letter shapes for a personalised message or to spell out the names of cheeses – think of it as cheese board scrabble for your guests!

All the biscuits are beautifully packaged and can be bought by contacting Rachel via her website or at the many markets and fayres she attends in the Cambridge area.

**The Biscuit Jar**
Tel: +44 (0)7919 418 396
Email: rachel@thebiscuitjar.co.uk
www.thebiscuitjar.co.uk
www.facebook.com/thebiscuitjar

One of the great benefits and satisfactions of shopping independently is the ability to buy something to reflect your individuality. Struggling to find unique pieces to decorate her home with, Wendy, founder of Design Essentials, took her search direct to Indonesia from where she now personally imports her own selection of beautiful home accessories and makes them available in the UK for others to purchase.

The majority of the items Wendy chooses are hand-made using sustainable materials and all have a contemporary feel. The lighting pieces are selected in particular for their ability to not only look stunning but also to create a mood and are like sculptures in their own right. Wood and metal are constantly featured materials along with glass and ceramics in a collection that extends to both large and small sculptural pieces, vases and wall hangings.

Some of Wendy's collection is permanently on display in various shops in the area including Modish Shoes (Green Street, Cambridge) and Goddards Interiors (in Saffron Walden). She also holds regular evening events where all the pieces can be viewed and enjoyed along with a glass of wine and something to nibble. As well as the Indonesian collection, Wendy uses these events as an opportunity to showcase work by local artists and also on-hand is an interior designer – there to offer advice and useful tips on all things design-related.

### Design Essentials

Tel: +44 (0)781 3840 402

Email: wendy@designessentials.org.uk

www.facebook.com/designessentials.home

www.designessentials.org.uk

Inder and Nick moved from London to Cambridge in 2010 with the dream of building an Indian catering business which would truly be able to show the diverse range of dishes and flavours that Indian cuisine really has to offer.

Using local suppliers wherever possible and taking daily delivery of responsibly-farmed meat (such as free-range chicken and lamb from Suffolk), fish and vegetables – Inder combines the freshest, seasonal produce with her true passion for home cooked Indian food, to produce a healthier and tastier alternative to traditional takeaways and tandoori restaurants.

Inder's seasonal menus are created to introduce customers to very traditional dishes from the Indian subcontinent, throughout the year. Starters are typical street foods and snacks, and main courses and sides bring together a wide variety of curries, dishes and pickles that are cooked in homes across India. The number of dishes on each menu is carefully controlled to allow Inder and her team to prepare them from scratch, as opposed to the one-sauce-fits all approach so often used. Indeed, the food created in Inder's Kitchen has led to the business being selected as one of just three finalists in the 2012 BBC Food and Farming Awards in the category of best takeaway/street food.

In addition to the seasonal menu, Inder also cooks bi-weekly specials and mild children's meals for younger diners. The latest menu, specials and kids options are always available on Inder's website where you can also place orders and book preferred delivery times in advance. Delivery is free of charge to all areas of Cambridge, Trumpington, Granchester, Girton, Teversham, Fen Ditton, the Shelfords and Stapleford.

### Inder's Kitchen

43 Clifton Road, Cambridge CB1 7ED
Tel: +44 (0)1223 211333
Email: info@inderskitchen.com
www.inderskitchen.com
Mon – Fri: 12pm-10pm (last orders)
Sat & Sun: 5pm-10pm (last orders)

*The freshness and diversity of true Indian food*

## JJ Vincent Ceramic Animals Owner: Trevor JJ Vincent

'I won't be around forever but it's nice to think that my fingerprints might be!'

JJ was born, raised and has worked in Cambridge all his life. He has been involved with graphic design and model making for most of that time. Major local clients included Addenbrooke's hospital (it's his 3D map you see as you enter the hospital site). Tatties Restaurant and The Cambridge Corn Exchange, both utilised his illustrated logos for more than 20 years.

More recently JJ, has begun making a name for himself producing ceramic animal sculptures.

He works in a variety of styles, reflecting different levels of anatomical accuracy – some pieces are fairly closely studied and more 'correct', whilst others can be highly simplified or stylised and a bit surreal. Either way, you can be sure that each face has individual character and will tell a story.

Whether it is for sculpting domestic pets, farm or wild animals, he always welcomes enquiries for special animal commissions, including exclusive pet portraits.

JJ is a member of Anglian Potters and regularly exhibits in Cambridge at The Emmanuel College Summer show and The All Saints Church Christmas show.

His work can be viewed at numerous UK galleries and he regularly exhibits during Cambridge Open Studios, when you can see the full range of his work. Larger, one-off pieces are becoming a speciality, often utilising his previous exhibition experience working in wood and metal to capture a narrative.

For details about commissioning a ceramic animal sculpture see JJ's website or follow the updates on his blog.

JJ Vincent Ceramic Animals
Tel: +44 (0)1223 240996
Email: jj@jjvincent.com
www.jjvincent.com
www.ceramicanimalsculptures.blogspot.co.uk

Just six months into starting her business, Carri Pavitt was awarded Gold at the British Pie Awards 2012 for her chicken and mushroom pies. These annual awards provide recognition for the quality, heritage and craftsmanship of British pie makers and knowing the passion Carri has for all these aspects, it's a fitting accolade for Pavitt's Pies to win.

Putting her own name to the pies has made Carri even more committed to making sure they are the best they can possibly be. A long time was spent developing the pastry – she uses flaky pastry, all made by hand, for its flavour and form, which has thin layers making it light and crispy. Time and effort has also gone in to sourcing the best ingredients for filling her pies – all of which contain no preservatives. Working in collaboration with local companies, Carri buys her meat from Andrew Northrop Butchers, including Label Anglais chickens, Riverside Beef for her beef and ale pies and she has worked with local brewers Moonshine Brewery to find the best ale to use in these too.

Other delicious filling combinations include pork and chorizo, mushroom, onion and thyme, and cheese and onion and the pies come in different sizes – canapé and snack pies, individual dinner pies and family sharing pies. Carri's local stockists are Balzano's Delicatessen, Burwash Manor, Gog Magog Hills, The Hopbine and Urban Larder, but you can also order via her website and have yummy pies delivered to you. Carri also caters for events and parties, accompanying serving pies with mash and onion gravy or handmade salads.

**Pavitt's Pies of Cambridge**
Tel: +44 (0)7950 336059
Email: carri.pavitt@pavitts-pies.co.uk
www.pavitts-pies.co.uk

# Events

# Cambridge Film Festival

Cambridge Film Festival was established in 1977 and is the country's third-longest running film festival after Edinburgh and London. Taking place each year, in the second half of September and running for ten days, the Festival brings together an eclectic mix of world, independent and mainstream cinema, new and as-yet unreleased titles (including submissions from filmmakers), documentaries, revivals of classic titles, themed seasons, short films and special events.

With its intimate surroundings and friendly atmosphere (no red carpets here – filmmakers mingle happily with audience members in the bar) it regularly attracts major names in cinema. In 2011 for example, the Festival opening night film – Tinker Tailor Soldier Spy – was attended by stars Gary Oldman and John Hurt, director Tomas Alfredson and screenwriter Peter Straughan. It has also been a place to discover new cinematic talent – Christopher Nolan had one of his very first short films shown here.

Regular features at the Festival include a special selection of the latest in German Contemporary Cinema (co-programmed by German director Monik Treut), Shortfusion (programmes of selected short films submitted by filmmakers from around the world), Microcinema (works by artist-filmmakers) and the Family Film Festival consisting of special, family-friendly screenings of TV favourites old and new, geared to those with very young children and providing shorter screenings (for those shorter attention spans) and a fun, relaxed environment with activities before and after the film.

Screenings take place mainly at the Arts Picturehouse in St Andrew's Street, but over the years the Festival has established a reputation for holding screenings (often free) in some unusual locations, including many of Cambridge's unique open spaces. Each year, popular screenings are held at Grantchester Meadows, in Magdalene Street and at Jesus Green Lido.

**Cambridge Film Festival**
c/o Arts Picturehouse
38-39 St Andrew's Street
Cambridge CB2 3AR
Tel: +44 (0)1223 500082
www.cambridgefilmfestival.org.uk

Photography © Tom Catchesides

# Cambridge Folk Festival

Set in the beautiful parkland setting of Cherry Hinton Hall on the outskirts of the city, Cambridge Folk Festival is one of the highlights in the city's calendar. Attracting 14,000 people across four days in late July, the Festival draws on its unrivalled 47 year musical heritage, combining it with the brand new, quirky, up and coming and unsung, to create a unique event each year.

It all began back in autumn 1964, when Cambridge City Council decided to hold a music festival the next summer and asked Ken Woollard, a local firefighter and socialist political activist, to help organise it. Woollard had been inspired by a documentary – Jazz On A Summer's Day, about the 1958 Newport Jazz Festival. On the very first Festival bill, squeezed in as a late addition, was a young Paul Simon who had just released I Am A Rock. The festival's popularity quickly grew, evolving over the years into one of the most well-loved and best regarded of its kind.

Today it features four stages – Main Stage, Stage 2, Club Tent and more recently, The Den – a hugely popular emerging talent stage. Artists over the years have included Laura Marling, Richard Thompson, Newton Faulkener, Jimmy Cliff, Mary Chapin Carpenter, Bellowhead, The Divine Comedy, Gillian Welch, Mumford and Sons, Rumer, Robert Cray, Christy Moore, Kate Rusby, Nanci Griffith, The Unthanks, Seasick Steve, Imelda May, Femi Kuti, Seth Lakeman, Nic Jones and many others.

**Cambridge Folk Festival**

Tel: +44 (0)1223 457555

Email: admin.cornex@cambridge.gov.uk

www.cambridgefolkfestival.co.uk

*the Glastonbury of the folk calendar*

# Cambridge Music Festival Director: Justin Lee

With a new Director comes a new direction for the Cambridge Music Festival. Embracing three areas Cambridge is renowned for worldwide – music, education and technology – the Festival brings all these together in its new annual format. Held every November in a number of locations throughout the City, the Festival features world-class artists in orchestral, choral and chamber music concerts, alongside a programme of education and free events as well as innovative outdoor sound/light projections on central Cambridge landmarks.

Established in 1991 to mark the bicentenary of the death of Mozart, the Festival has grown in size and reputation. Acclaimed artists on the programme for the 2012 Cambridge Music Festival included Murray Perahia (director and piano), the Academy of St Martin in the Fields, Andreas Scholl (countertenor), Alison Balsom (trumpet), and the Tallis Scholars. The Festival's education and community work has also attracted particular acclaim for helping to engage young people in music making. This work was nominated in 2006 for the Festival's 'Orchestra in a Village' project, in the RPS (Royal Philharmonic Society) Music Awards. The awards celebrate creativity, excellence and understanding in classical music making throughout the UK, and the Festival is always looking for innovative ways to bring wider participation and appreciation of this form of music.

While much of the education work is aimed at young people in the North and East of Cambridge, many stunning buildings around the City are home to the Festival's programme of concerts such as King's College chapel, St Andrews Street Baptist Church, St John's College chapel, Trinity College chapel, the West Road Concert Hall and the Corn Exchange.

**Cambridge Music Festival**
Tel: +44 (0)1223 357851
Email: info@cammusic.co.uk
www.cammusic.co.uk

*Photo credits from top left:*
*Chris Dunlop / EMI; Nana Watanabe; Daniel Oi*

Alison Balsom
*Trumpet*

Murray Perahia
*Piano*

King's Junior Voices

# Cambridge Wordfest Festival Director: Cathy Moore

Just over ten years ago, Cathy Moore was talking to local author Ali Smith about the absence of a literary festival in Cambridge. They agreed that it seemed crazy that such a renowned seat of learning should lack a public space for debate, exchange and reflection. Cycling along, with thoughts of the conversation buzzing through her mind, the kernel of the first Cambridge Wordfest had formed by the time Cathy got home.

Working from her kitchen table and with the help of a small band of friends and volunteers, she began to pull this first festival together – a two-day celebration with 24 events including readings from Jackie Kay and Ali Smith, Will Hutton, Polly Toynbee, Nicci French and Francesca Simon – plus 950 ticket sales.

Today Cambridge Wordfest consists of two festivals per year, one in spring, the other in winter, with the spring 2012 festival staging 75 events and workshops and almost 9,000 tickets sold to see and hear from the likes of Iain Banks, Julian Clary, Michael Portillo, Grace Dent, Charley Boorman and Ian Rankin. And it's not just for grown-ups as there's a vibrant programme of events for children too.

But although the festival has grown so successfully,

Cambridge Wordfest has managed to retain its initial intimacy and vivacity and continues to delight its festival-goers by bringing the best in new and established writers to the historic and beautiful city of Cambridge.

**Cambridge Wordfest**
Festival Office
7 Downing Place, Cambridge CB3 2EL
Tel: +44 (0)1223 515335
Email: admin@cambridgewordfest.co.uk
www.cambridgewordfest.co.uk

*unique in offering inspiration and intimacy in equal measures*

# Mill Road Winter Fair

The Mill Road Winter Fair celebrates the quirky community spirit and multiculturalism that make this road so special. Always held on the first Saturday in December, it's an important event in the seasonal calendar – bringing many thousands of people to the area, raising the profile of Mill Road, increasing awareness of its many and diverse businesses and community groups and generally providing a colourful and fun-filled time for visitors.

With the road closed between East Road and Coleridge Road, visitors to the fair can stroll along the street and see the amazing variety of what is on offer. Crammed full of independent shops, Mill Road is truly diverse, both in what can be found for sale or to eat and in terms of who is selling or preparing it. Chinese and Korean restaurants and supermarkets, cyber cafés and coffee houses, Indian restaurants, an Italian delicatessen, North African, Adriatic and Turkish restaurants and shops selling organic and locally-produced food and other wears sit alongside antique shops, book shops, bike shops, a butchers, a bakers and there's probably even a candlestick-maker!

And as well as this variety of shops, the fair hosts a food fair, art show and craft stalls and sees street performers congregate to entertain the public. Musicians, dancers and other artists all gather to perform along the road and in marquees, pubs and clubs. Truly something for everyone!

**Mill Road Winter Fair**

C/O The Post Office, 100A Mill Road
Cambridge CB1 2BD
Tel: +44 (0)7982 810 343
Email: info@millroadwinterfair.org
www.millroadwinterfair.org

*A perfect mixture of organised spontaniety!*

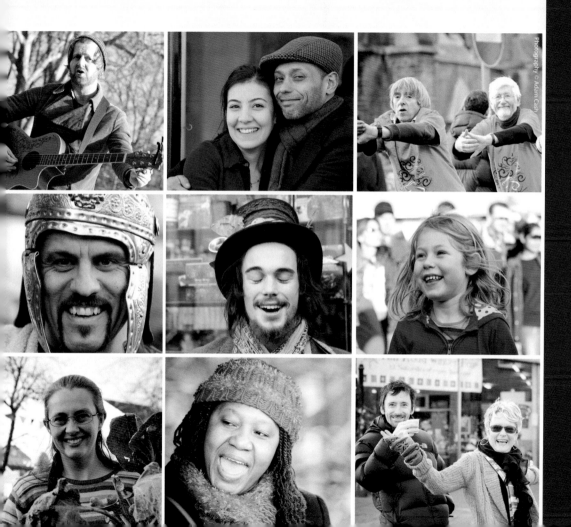

Photography © Adam Cash

# Strawberry Fair

On the first Saturday in June, Midsummer Common is transformed in to a colourful concoction of music, art, performance, stalls and fun as residents and visitors gather together to celebrate at the annual Strawberry Fair.

Throughout the day, across seven stages, the Fair dances to sounds from the spectrum of 'pop' music. From folk to funk, from soulful solo acoustic players to hard rocking bands, plus djs – most musical tastes are well catered for. Fair-goers can also enjoy a variety of spoken word performances, poetry and arts activities, many especially for children and young people. The Cambridge Community Circus has been a particular favourite in recent years.

And no fair would be complete without an assortment of crafts, clothes and culinary delights on sale. As much as possible, the Fair aims to offer the products and produce of those that share its ethical values and local independent spirit. There is also plenty of space to relax and enjoy calmer pursuits, including the Green Area, traditionally the residence of herbalists and healers, and the Meditation Zone. Several local community action groups also have stalls in this area.

The Fair, which has been a feature of the city for almost forty years, is run entirely by volunteers. The Fair is not-for-profit, non-political and independent. It is also self-funding, raising money mainly through selling stall space and running benefit gigs and other fundraising events throughout the year.

**Strawberry Fair**

PO Box 104, Cambridge CB4 1WZ

www.strawberry-fair.org.uk

Directory

Independent Individual & In this bag

# Independent Cambridge Directory

As well as the fantastic independents we have featured, there are many more great places to discover in and around Cambridge. They are all listed here by category (some appear in more than one) and are also in a searchable database at *www.independent-cambridge.co.uk*

*Indies featured in this book are highlighted in green, together with the page number.*

If you know of any that you think should be included that we have missed, we would love to know, so please drop us an email at *info@independent-cambridge.co.uk* and we'll add them to the database.

## ANTIQUES

**Cambs Antique Centre**
1-2 Dales Brewery
Gwydir Street
Cambridge CB1 2LJ
+44 (0)1223 356391
www.twitter.com/cambsantiques

**Eastwind Ltd, Cambridge**    116
224 Mill Road
Cambridge CB1 3NS
+44 (0)1223 471262

**Gabor Cossa Antiques**
34 Trumpington Street
Cambridge CB2 1QY
+44 (0)1223 356049
www.gaborcossa.co.uk

**The Hive**
3 Dales Brewery
Gwydir Street
Cambridge CB1 2LJ
+44 (0)1223 300269
www.hiveantiques.co.uk

**John Beazor Antiques**
78/80 Regent Street
Cambridge CB2 1DP
+44 (0)1223 355178
www.johnbeazorantiques.co.uk

**The Old Chemist Antique Shop**
206 Mill Road
Cambridge CB1 3NF
+44 (0)1223 247324

## ART, CRAFTS AND GALLERIES

**Byard Art**
14 King's Parade
Cambridge CB2 1SJ
+44 (0)1223 464646
www.byardart.co.uk

**Cambridge Art Salon**    138
29 Cromwell Road
Cambridge CB1 3EB
+44 (0)1223 244391
www.cambridgeartsalon.org.uk

**Cambridge Contemporary Art**    42
6 Trinity Street
Cambridge CB2 1SU
+44 (0)1223 324 222
www.cambridgegallery.co.uk

**Cambridge Contemporary Crafts**    88
5 Bene't Street
Cambridge CB2 3QN
+44 (0)1223 361200
www.cambridgecrafts.co.uk

**Cambridge Craft Market at All Saints Garden**    36
All Saints Garden, Trinity Street
Cambridge CB2 1TQ
+44 (0)7769 628788
www.cambridge-craft-market.co.uk

**Cambridge Creative Network**
www.cambridgecreativenetwork.co.uk

**CamCreative**
www.camcreative.net

**Cam Photographers**
www.camphotographers.wix.com

**Cheffins Fine Art Auctioneers**
Clifton House, Clifton Road
Cambridge CB1 7EA
+44 (0)1223 213343
www.cheffins.co.uk

**Eastwind Ltd, Cambridge**    116
224 Mill Road
Cambridge CB1 3NS
+44 (0)1223 471262

**Frameworks**    104
170 Mill Road
Cambridge CB1 3LP
+44 (0)1223 213092/778817
www.frameworks-cambridge.co.uk

**General and Sunday Markets**    76
Market Square
Cambridge CB2
+44 (0)1223 457000
www.cambridge.gov.uk/markets

**Harry Gray Sculptor**    140
Studio 53A, St Philips Road
Cambridge CB1 3DA
+44 (0)1223 410751
www.harrygray.co.uk

**JJ Vincent Ceramic Animal Sculptures**    158
www.jjvincent.com

**Jo Clark Design**
www.joclarkdesign.co.uk

**Katharina Klug Ceramics**
+44 (0)7765 245758
www.katharina.klug-art.com

**Kettle's Yard**  12
Castle Street
Cambridge CB3 0AQ
+44 (0)1223 748100
www.kettlesyard.co.uk

**The Lawson Gallery**
7/8 King's Parade
Cambridge CB2 1SJ
+44 (0)1223 313970
www.lawson-gallery.com

**Makers' Gallery**
3-4 Hope Street Yard
Mill Road
Cambridge CB1 3NA
+44 (0)1223 414870
www.makersgallery.co.uk

**Open Studios**
www.camopenstudios.co.uk

**Podarok**
12 Bene't Street
Cambridge CB2 3PT
+44 (0)1223 314411
www.podarok.co.uk

**Primavera**  84
10 King's Parade
Cambridge CB2 1SJ
+44 (0)1223 357708
www.primaverauk.com

**Primavera**  18
13 Magdalene Street
Cambridge CB3 0AF
+44 (0)1223 357708
www.primaverauk.com

**Primavera**  130
6 Wellington Court
Cambridge, CB1 1HZ
+44 (0)1223 357708
www.primaverauk.com

**Rowan**  128
40 Humberstone Road
Cambridge CB4 1JG
+44 (0)1223 566027
www.rowanhumberstone.co.uk

**St Barnabas Press**  132
Coldhams Road
Cambridge CB1 3EW
+44 (0)1223 413792
stbarnabaspress.webplus.net

**White House Arts**  124
72 Fen Road
Cambridge CB4 1UN
+44 (0)1223 420018
www.whitehousearts.co.uk

**Williams Art**
5 Dales Brewery
Gwydir Street
Cambridge CB1 2LJ
+44 (0)1223 311687
www.williamsart.co.uk

## BIKES

**Blazing Saddles**
102 Cherry Hinton Road
Cambridge CB1 7AJ
+44 (0)1223 650045
www.blazing-saddles-cambridge.co.uk

**Ben Hayward Cycles**
69 Trumpington Street
Cambridge CB2 1RJ
+44 (0)1223 352294
www.benhaywardcycles.co.uk

**Camcycles**
92 Mill Road
Cambridge CB1 2BD
+44 (0)1223 500988
www.camcycles.co.uk

**Claud Butler Cambridge**
171 Mill Road
Cambridge CB1 3AN
+44 (0)1223 576545

**The Cycle Repair Shop**
26 Mill Road
Cambridge CB1 2AD
+44 (0)1223 360028
www.thecyclerepairshop.co.uk

**Electric Transport Shop**
Hope Street Yard
Mill Road
Cambridge CB1 3NA
+44 (0)1223 247410
www.electricbikesales.co.uk

**Primo Cycles**
5/7 Jesus Lane
Cambridge CB5 8BA
+44 (0)1223 500502
www.primocycles.co.uk

**The School Run Centre
(Dutch Bikes)** 112
Hope Street Yard
Mill Road,
Cambridge CB1 3NA
+44 (0)7772 738899
www.schoolruncentre.co.uk

**Station Cycles Cambridge**
Station Buildings
Station Road
Cambridge CB3 2JW
+44 (0)1223 307125

**Townsends Light
Blue Cycle Centre**
72 Chesterton Road
Cambridge CB4 1EP
+44 (0)1223 315845
www.lightblue.co.uk

**University Cycles**
9 Victoria Avenue
Cambridge CB4 1EG
+44 (0)1223 355517

## BOOKS

**The Angel Bookshop**
2 Bene't Street
Cambridge CB2 3QN
+44 (0)1223 316244
www.angelbookshop.co.uk

**Books for Amnesty Cambridge**
46 Mill Road
Cambridge CB1 2AS
+44 (0)1223 362496
www.amnesty.org.uk

**Cambridge International
Book Centre**
42 Hills Road
Cambridge CB2 1LA
+44 (0)1223 365400
www.eflbooks.co.uk

**Cambridge University
Press Bookshop** 44
1 Trinity Street
Cambridge CB2 1SZ
+44 (0)1223 333333
www.cambridge.org/uk/
bookshop

**G David Bookseller** 82
16 St Edward's Passage
Cambridge CB2 3PJ
+44 (0)1223 354619
www.gdavidbookseller.co.uk

**General and Sunday
Markets** 76
Market Square
Cambridge CB2
+44 (0)1223 457000
www.cambridge.gov.uk/markets

**The Haunted Bookshop**
9 St Edward's Passage
Cambridge CB2 3PJ
+44 (0)1223 312913
www.sarahkeybooks.co.uk

**Plurabelle Books Ltd**
Homerton Business Centre
Purbeck Road
Cambridge CB2 8QL
+44 (0)1223 415671
www.plurabellebooks.com

## CAFÉS

**Adilia's Norfolk St Bakery** 136
89 Norfolk Street
Cambridge CB1 2LD
+44 (0)1223 660163

**Balzano's Deli and Café** 146
204 Cherry Hinton Road
Cambridge CB1 7AW
+44 (0)1223 246168

**Black Cat Café**
2, The Broadway, Mill Road
Cambridge CB1 3AH
+44 (0)1223 248972
www.blackcatcafecambridge.co.uk

**The Box Café** 134
47 Norfolk Street
Cambridge CB1 2LD
www.theboxcafe.co.uk

**Bridges Patisserie**
20 Bridge Street
Cambridge CB2 1UF
+44(0)1223 300800
www.bridgespatisserie.co.uk

**Burwash Manor**
New Road, Barton
Cambridge CB23 7EY
www.burwashmanor.com

**Café Brazil**
64 Mill Road
Cambridge CB1 2AS
+44 (0)1223 301400
www.cafebrazil.co.uk

**Café de Paris**
68 Mill Road
Cambridge CB1 2AS
+44 (0)1223 300850

**Café on the Round**
16 Round Church Street
Cambridge CB5 8AD
+44 (0)1223 308279
www.cafeontheround.co.uk

**CB1**
32 Mill Road
Cambridge CB1 2AD
+44 (0)1223 576306
www.cb1.com

**CB2**
5/7 Norfolk Street
Cambridge CB1 2LD
+44 (0)1223 508503
www.cb2bistro.com

**Chapter 2 Café &
Patisserie**
60 Hills Road
Cambridge CB2 1LA
+44 (0)1223 353030

**Clowns**
54 King Street
Cambridge CB1 1LN
+44 (0)1223 355711

**Cornerstone Café**
St Philips Church Centre
185 Mill Road
Cambridge CB1 3AN
+44(0)1223 213656
www.papworth.org.uk/centres

Fitzbillies                                  90
52 Trumpington Street
Cambridge CB2 1RG
+44 (0)1223 352500
www.fitzbillies.com

**Harriets Café Tearooms**
16 & 17 Green Street
Cambridge CB2 3JU
+44 (0)1223 356443
www.harrietscafetearooms.co.uk

**Hot Numbers**
Unit 6 Dale's Brewery, Gwydir St
Cambridge CB1 2LJ
+44 (0)1223 359966
www.hotnumberscoffee.co.uk

**Indigo Coffee House**
8 Saint Edwards Passage
Cambridge CB2 3PJ

Le Gros Franck                              142
57 Hills Road
Cambridge CB2 1NT
+44 (0)1223 565560
www.legrosfranck.com

Limoncello                                  110
212 Mill Road
Cambridge CB1 3NF
+44 (0)1223 507036
www.limoncello.co.uk

**Michaelhouse Café**
St. Michael's Church, Trinity St
Cambridge CB2 1SU
+44 (0)1223 309147
www.michaelhousecafe.co.uk

Nord                                         26
36 Bridge Street
Cambridge CB2 1UW
+44 (0)1223 321884
www.nordesign.co.uk

**The Orchard Tea Garden**
45-47 Mill Way, Grantchester
Cambridge CB3 9ND
+44 (0)1223 551125
www.orchard-grantchester.com

**Otto Café**
198 Mill Road
Cambridge CB1 3NF
+44 (0)1223 359403
(also Regent Street)

**Rainbow Café**
9a King's Parade
Cambridge CB2 1SJ
+44 (0)1223 321551
www.rainbowcafe.co.uk

**Stickybeaks**
42 Hobson Street
Cambridge CB1 1NL
+44 (0)1223 359397
www.stickybeakscafe.co.uk

Ta Bouche                                    70
10-15 Market Passage
Cambridge CB2 3PF
+44 (0)1223 462277
www.tabouche.co.uk

**Trockel Ulmann & Freunde**
13 Pembroke Street
Cambridge CB2 3QY
+44 (0)1223 460923

Urban Larder                                106
9, The Broadway, Mill Road
Cambridge CB1 3AH
+44 (0)1223 212462
www.urbanlarder.co.uk

## CULTURE AND LEARNING

**The ACE Foundation**
The Granary, Bury Farm
Bury Road, Stapleford
Cambridge CB22 5BP
+44 (0)1223 845599
www.acefoundation.org.uk

Alliance Française
de Cambridge                                142
60 Hills Road
Cambridge CB2 1LA
+44(0)1223 561854
www.alliance-cam.co.uk

**Cambridge Cookery School**
Unit 9D, The Imre Building
Homerton Business Centre
Purbeck Road
Cambridge CB2 8HN
+44 (0)1223 247620
www.cambridgecookeryschool.com

**Cat, Fish etc LLP**
www.catfish-etc.com

**Fitzwilliam Museum**
Trumpington Street
Cambridge CB2 1RB
+44 (0)1223 332900
www.fitzmuseum.cam.ac.uk

**Folk Museum** 14
2/3 Castle Street
Cambridge CB3 0AQ
+44 (0)1223 355159
www.folkmuseum.org.uk

**Kettle's Yard** 12
Castle Street
Cambridge CB3 0AQ
+44 (0)1223 748100
www.kettlesyard.co.uk

**Rowan** 128
40 Humberstone Road
Cambridge CB4 1JG
+44 (0)1223 566027
www.rowanhumberstone.co.uk

**St Barnabas Press** 132
Coldhams Road
Cambridge CB1 3EW
+44 (0)1223 413792
stbarnabaspress.webplus.net

**White House Arts** 124
72 Fen Road
Cambridge CB4 1UN
+44 (0)1223 420018
www.whitehousearts.co.uk

## EVENTS

**Cambridge Comedy Festival**
www.cambridgecomedyfestival.com

**Cambridge Film Festival** 164
+44 (0)1223 500082
www.cambridgefilmfestival.org.uk

**Cambridge Folk Festival** 166
+44 (0)1223 457555
www.cambridgefolkfestival.co.uk

**Cambridge Music Festival** 168
+44 (0)1223 357851
www.cammusic.co.uk

**Cambridge Shakespeare Festival**
+44 (0)7955 218824
www.cambridgeshakespeare.com

**Cambridge Summer Music Festival**
+44 (0)1223 894161
www.cambridgesummermusic.com

**Mill Road Winter Fair** 172
www.millroadwinterfair.org

**Strawberry Fair** 174
www.strawberry-fair.org.uk

**Wordfest** 170
+44 (0)1223 515335
www.cambridgewordfest.co.uk

## FASHION

**Anthony (for him)** 38
18 Trinity Street
Cambridge CB2 1TB
+44 (0)1223 360592
www.anthonymenswear.co.uk

**Arthur Shepherd (for him)**
32 Trinity Street
Cambridge CB2 1TB
+44 (0)1223 353962
www.arthurshepherd.co.uk

**Baska (for her)** 20
18 Magdalene Street
Cambridge CB3 0AF
+44 (0)1223 353800
www.baska.co.uk

**Boudoir Femme (for her)**
2 King Street
Cambridge CB1 1LN
+44 (0)1223 323000
www.boudoirfemme.co.uk

**Bowns & Bis (for her)** 24
24 & 25 Magdalene Street
Cambridge CB3 0AF
+44 (0)1223 302000
www.bownscambridge.com

**Burwash Manor**
New Road, Barton
Cambridge CB23 7EY
www.burwashmanor.com

**Cambridge Raincoat Company**
www.cambridgeraincoats.co.uk

**Cambridge Satchel Company Ltd**
+44(0)1223 833050
www.cambridgesatchel.co.uk

**Cuckoo (for her)** 78
4 St Mary's Passage
Cambridge CB2 3PQ
+44 (0)1223 364345
www.cuckooclothing.co.uk

**Curious Orange (for him & her)**
+44 (0)7942 765313
www.curious-orange.com

**Dogfish (for him)**
29 Trinity Street
Cambridge CB2 1TB
+44 (0)1223 327959
www.dogfishmen.co.uk

**General and Sunday Markets** 76
Market Square
Cambridge CB2
+44 (0)1223 457000
www.cambridge.gov.uk/markets

**Giles & Co**
4 Trinity Street
Cambridge CB2 1SU
+44 (0)1223 366841
www.universitystore.co.uk

**Jemporium Vintage**
Unit 61, The Grafton Centre
Cambridge CB1 1PS
www.jemporiumvintage.co.uk

**Le Reve Lingerie**
6 Bene't Street
Cambridge CB2 3QN
+44 (0)1223 328111
www.lereve-lingerie.com

**Lilac Rose (for her)**
71 Bridge Street
Cambridge CB2 1UR
+44 (0)1223 363330

**Mayhem (for him & her)**
41 Sidney Street
Cambridge CB2 3HX
+44 (0)1223 322030
www.mayhemuk.co.uk

**Mia Sposa (bridal & for him)**
4 Homerton Street
Cambridge CB2 8NX
+44 (0)1223 213770
www.miasposacambridge.co.uk

**Modish Shoes**　　　54
3 Green Street
Cambridge CB2 3JU
+44 (0)1223 354436
www.modishonline.co.uk

**Nomads
(ethnic clothing)**　　86
5 King's Parade
Cambridge CB2 1SJ
+44 (0)1223 324588
www.nomads.uk.com

**One World is Enough
(ethnic clothing)**
30B Bridge Street
Cambridge CB2 1UJ
+44 (0)1223 361102
www.one-world-is-enough.net

**Open Air
(outdoor clothing)**　　50
11 Green Street
Cambridge CB2 3JU
+44 (0)1223 324666
www.openair.co.uk

**Petrus (for him & her)**　　32
67 Bridge Street
Cambridge CB2 1UR
+44 (0)1223 352588
www.petrusdesign.co.uk

**Prohibido Lingerie**
5 All Saint's Passage
Cambridge CB2 3LS
+44 (0)1223 316553
www.prohibido.co.uk

**Rejuvinate**
28 Hills Road
Cambridge CB2 1LA
+44 (0)1223 360949
www.rejuvinateshop.co.uk

**Rosie's Vintage (for her)**　58
18 King Street
Cambridge CB1 1LN
+44 (0)1223 511696
www.rosiesvintage.co.uk

**Sandra Kent (for her)**
12 Rose Crescent
Cambridge CB2 3LL
+44 (0)1223 360709

**Seven Wolves (for him)**
4 Bridge Street
Cambridge CB2 1UA
+44 (0)1223 366032
www.sevenwolves.co.uk

**The Sheep Shop**
72 Beche Road
Cambridge CB5 8HU
+44 (0)1223 311268
www.sheepshopcambridge.co.uk

**Sundaes (shoes)**　　52
36 Green Street
Cambridge CB2 3JX
+44 (0)1223 361536
www.sundaes-shoes.co.uk

**The Tailor's Cat
(bridalwear)**
2 Sussex Street
Cambridge CB1 1PA
+44 (0)1223 366700
www.cambridge-bridalwear.co.uk

**Tailor & Cutter**
7 All Saints Passage
Cambridge CB3 2LS
+44 (0)1223 300677
www.tailorandcutter.co.uk

**Talking T's**　　28
37 Bridge Street
Cambridge CB2 1UW
+44 (0)1223 302411
www.t-shirts.co.uk

**This is Cambridge**
+44 (0)776 6741 721
www.this-is-cambridge.co.uk

**Troon (for her)**
16 King's Parade
Cambridge CB2 1SP
+44 (0)1223 360274
www.troondesignerclothing.com

**Vida Moda
(plus sizes for her)**
+44 (0)8456 806 524
www.vidamoda.co.uk

## FLORISTS

**The Flower House**   22
23 Magdalene Street
Cambridge CB3 0AF
+44 (0)1223 364500
www.theflowerhouse.co.uk

## FOOD

**Adilia's Norfolk
Street Bakery**   136
89 Norfolk Street
Cambridge CB1 2LD
+44 (0)1223 660163

**Afternoon Tease**
+44 (0)7810 202673
www.afternoontease.co.uk

**Al-Amin**   98
100a-102a Mill Road
Cambridge CB1 2BD
+44 (0)1223 576396/7
www.alamin.co.uk

**Andrew Northrop
Butchers**   102
114 Mill Road
Cambridge CB1 2BQ
+44 (0)1223 354779

**Arjuna Wholefoods**
12 Mill Road
Cambridge CB1 2AD
+44 (0)1223 364845
www.arjunawholefoods.co.uk

**A Waller & Son (butchers)**
15 Victoria Avenue
Cambridge CB4 1EG
+44 (0)1223 350972

**Balzano's Deli & Café**   146
204 Cherry Hinton Road
Cambridge CB1 7AW
+44 (0)1223 246168

**Bellina Chocolate House**
8 Bridge Street
Cambridge CB2 1UA
+44 (0)1223 322352
www.chocolatehouse.co.uk

**The Biscuit Jar**   152
+44 (0)7919 418396
www.thebiscuitjar.co.uk

**Burwash Manor**
New Road, Barton
Cambridge CB23 7EY
www.burwashmanor.com

**The Cambridge
Cheese Company**
All Saints Passage
Cambridge CB2 3LS
+44 (0)1223 328672
www.cambridgecheese.com

**Cambridge Cookery School**
Unit 9D, The Imre Building
Homerton Business Centre
Purbeck Road
Cambridge CB2 8HN
+44 (0)1223 247620
www.cambridgecookeryschool.com

**Cambridge Farmers' Outlet**
8 Lensfield Road
Cambridge CB2 1EG
+44 (0)7885 686 947

**Chocolat Chocolat**
21 Saint Andrew's Street
Cambridge CB2 3AX
+44 (0)1223 778982
www.chocolatchocolat.co.uk

**Cho Mee**
108–110 Mill Road
Cambridge CB1 2BD
+44 (0)1223 354399
www.facebook.com/
ChoMeeSupermarketUK

**General and Sunday
Markets**   76
Market Square
Cambridge CB2
+44 (0)1223 457000
www.cambridge.gov.uk/markets

**Gog Magog Hills Farm Shop**
Heath Farm, Shelford Bottom
Cambridge CB22 3AD
+44 (0)1223 248 352
www.gogmagoghills.com

**Hilary's Greengrocers**
175a Mill Road
Cambridge CB1 3NF
+44 (0)1223 245309

**Limoncello**   110
212 Mill Road
Cambridge CB1 3NF
+44 (0)1223 507036
www.limoncello.co.uk

**Norfolk Street Deli**
67 Norfolk Street
Cambridge CB1 2LD
+44 (0)1223 302442

**Pavitt's Pies of
Cambridge**   160
+44 (0)7950 336059
www.pavittspies.co.uk

**Radmore Farm Shop**
30 Chesterton Road
Cambridge CB4 3AX
+44 (0)1223 361155
www.radmorefarmshop.co.uk

**The Sea Tree**   108
13/14 The Broadway, Mill Road
Cambridge CB1 3AH
+44 (0)1223 414349
www.theseatree.co.uk

**Shelford Delicatessen**
8a Woollards Lane, Great Shelford
Cambridge CB2 5LZ
+44 (0)1223 846129
www.shelforddeli.co.uk

**Urban Larder**   106
9, The Broadway, Mill Road
Cambridge CB1 3AH
+44 (0)1223 212462
www.urbanlarder.co.uk

## HAIR AND BEAUTY

**Bamboo**
202 Mill Road
Cambridge CB1 3NF
+44 (0)1223 502930
www.bamboohairdressing.co.uk

**Directors**
8 Green Street
Cambridge CB2 3JU
+44 (0)1223 311393
www.directors-hair.co.uk

**Elaje Hair & Beauty**
148 Hills Road
Cambridge CB2 8PB
+44 (0)1223 244888
www.elaje.co.uk

**Hairy Canary**
4 Wheeler Street
Cambridge CB2 3QE
+44 (0)1223 462817
www.hairycanary.net

**Ian James**
176 Mill Road
Cambridge CB1 3LP
+44 (0)1223 247962
www.ianjameshairdesign.co.uk

Julian                    62
56a King Street
Cambridge CB1 1LN
+44 (0)1223 361644

**Nutters**
10 Mill Road
Cambridge CB1 2AD
+44 (0)1223 365463
www.nuttershair.co.uk
(also Victoria Road)

**Scruffs**
68/69 Bridge Street
Cambridge CB2 1UR
+44 (0)1223 355358
www.scruffs.co.uk

**Secrets of Arabia**
12 Milton Road
Cambridge CB4 1JY
+44 (0)1223 366686
www.secretsofarabia.co.uk

**Stilo**
13 St John's Street
Cambridge CB2 1TW
+44 (0)1223 355339/352020
www.stilonuovo.co.uk

## HOME AND GIFTS

**Angel + Blume**
17 Emmanuel Road
Cambridge CB1 1JW
+44(0)1223 479 434
www.angelandblume.com

Ark                       80
2 St Mary's Passage
Cambridge CB2 3PQ
+44 (0)1223 363372
www.arkcambridge.co.uk

Breeze                    40
34 Trinity Street
Cambridge CB2 1TB
+44 (0)1223 354403
www.breeze.uk.com

**Burwash Manor**
New Road, Barton
Cambridge CB23 7EY
www.burwashmanor.com

**CallyCo**
7 Peas Hill
Cambridge CB2 3PP
+44 (0)1223 778744
www.callyco.com

**Cambridge Gift Shop**
Peas Hill
Cambridge CB2 3AD
+44(0)1223 313991
www.thecambridgegiftshop.com

**Crofthouse**
91 Cherry Hinton Road
Cambridge CB1 7BS
+44(0)1223 300858
www.ckbh.co.uk

Cutlacks                  118
264/268 Mill Road
Cambridge CB1 3NF
+44 (0)1223 246418
www.cutlacks.co.uk

Design Essentials         154
+44 (0)781 3840 402
www.designessentials.org.uk

Eastwind Ltd, Cambridge   116
224 Mill Road
Cambridge CB1 3NS
+44 (0)1223 471262

**H Gee**
94A Mill Road
Cambridge CB1 2BD
+44 (0)1223 358019

**Jo Clark Design**
www.joclarkdesign.co.uk

**Little Gift Shop
on the Corner**
18 Rose Crescent
Cambridge CB2 3LL
+44 (0)1223 315214
www.thelittlegiftshoponthe
corner.co.uk

**Nomads** 86
5 King's Parade
Cambridge CB2 1SJ
+44 (0)1223 324588
www.nomads.uk.com

**Nord** 26
36 Bridge Street
Cambridge CB2 1UW
+44 (0)1223 321884
www.nordesign.co.uk

**One World is Enough**
30B Bridge Street
Cambridge CB2 1UJ
+44 (0)1223 361102
www.one-world-is-enough.net

**Our Pretty House**
www.ourprettyhouse.co.uk

**Paint & Paper Emporium**
18b Chesterton Road
Cambridge CB4 3AX
+44 (0)1223 506136
www.paintandpaperemporium.com

**Podarok**
12 Bene't Street
Cambridge CB2 3PT
+44 (0)1223 314411
www.podarok.co.uk

**Primavera** 84
10 King's Parade
Cambridge CB2 1SJ
+44 (0)1223 357708
www.primaverauk.com

**Providence** 34
73 Bridge Street
Cambridge CB2 1UR
+44 (0)1223 506556
www.providenceuk.com

**Sandra Jane**
46-48 King Street
Cambridge CB1 1LN
+44 (0)1223 323211
www.sandrajane.co.uk

**This is Cambridge**
+44(0)776 6741 721
www.this-is-cambridge.co.uk

## HOTELS AND
## GUEST HOUSES

**Duke House**
1 Victoria Street
Cambridge CB1 1JP
+44 (0)1223 314773
www.dukehousecambridge.co.uk

**Hotel Felix**
Whitehouse Lane
Huntingdon Road
Cambridge CB3 0LX
+44(0)1223 277977
www.hotelfelix.co.uk

**The Varsity Hotel & Spa** 30
Thompson's Lane (off Bridge St)
Cambridge CB5 8AQ
+44 (0)1223 306030
www.thevarsityhotel.co.uk

**Warkworth House Hotel**
Warkworth Terrace
Cambridge CB1 1EE
+44(0)1223 363682
www.warkworthhouse.co.uk

## JEWELLERY

**Art Gecko**
15 Rose Crescent
Cambridge CB2 3LL
+44(0)1223 367483
www.artgeckojewellery.co.uk

**The Beaderie**
20 Magdalene Street
Cambridge CB3 0AF
www.thebeaderie.co.uk

**Cambridge
Contemporary Crafts** 88
5 Bene't Street
Cambridge CB2 3QN
+44 (0)1223 361200
www.cambridgecrafts.co.uk

**Cambridge Craft Market
at All Saints Garden** 36
All Saints Garden
Trinity Street
Cambridge CB2 1TQ
+44 (0)7769 628788
www.cambridge-craft-market.co.uk

**Catherine Jones**
9 Bridge Street
Cambridge CB2 1UA
+44 (0)1223 361596
www.catherinejones.com

**Cellini**
4 Rose Crescent
Cambridge CB2 3LL
+44 (0)1223 517700
www.cellini.co.uk

**Christopher Page Jewellers**
18 Kings Parade
Cambridge CB2 1SP
+44 (0)1223 313443
www.page-finejewellery.co.uk

**Eastwind Ltd, Cambridge** 116
224 Mill Road
Cambridge CB1 3NS
+44 (0)1223 471262

**General and Sunday
Markets** 76
Market Square, Cambridge CB2
+44 (0)1223 457000
www.cambridge.gov.uk/markets

**Graces Accessories**
6 All Saints Passage
Cambridge CB2 3LS
+44 (0)1223 301166
www.gracesaccessories.com

**Harriet Kelsall Jewellery Design Ltd**
6/7 Green Street
Cambridge CB2 3JU
+44 (0)1223 461333
www.hkjewellery.co.uk

**Nomads** 86
5 King's Parade
Cambridge CB2 1SJ
+44 (0)1223 324588
www.nomads.uk.com

**Our Pretty House**
www.ourprettyhouse.co.uk

**Podarok**
12 Bene't Street
Cambridge CB2 3PT
+44 (0)1223 314411
www.podarok.co.uk

**Powell & Bull**
31 Magdalene Street
Cambridge CB3 0AF
+44 (0)1223 462256
powellandbull.wordpress.com

**Primavera** 84
10 King's Parade
Cambridge CB2 1SJ
+44 (0)1223 357708
www.primaverauk.com

**S F Gautrey Jewellers**
48 Chesterton Road
Cambridge CB4 1EN
+44 (0)1223 352 518

**Trinity Street Jewellers**
31 Trinity Street
Cambridge CB2 1TB
+44 (0)1223 357 910
www.trinitystreetjewellers.co.uk

## JOINERY

**Linford Joinery** 144
217B Cherry Hinton Road
Cambridge CB1 7DA
Tel: +44 (0)7449 834098
https://www.facebook.com/
Linfordjoinerycambridge?fref=ts

## KIDS

**The Angel Bookshop**
2 Bene't Street
Cambridge CB2 3QN
+44 (0)1223 316244
www.angelbookshop.co.uk

**Ark** 80
2 St Mary's Passage
Cambridge CB2 3PQ
+44 (0)1223 363372
www.arkcambridge.co.uk

**The Biscuit Jar** 152
+44 (0)7919 418396
www.thebiscuitjar.co.uk

**Burwash Manor**
New Road, Barton
Cambridge CB23 7EY
www.burwashmanor.com

**Cambridge Toy Shop** 56
15/16 Sussex Street
Cambridge CB1 1PA
+44 (0)1223 309010
www.cambridgetoyshop.co.uk

**Cat, Fish etc LLP**
www.catfish-etc.com

**Inner Sanctum Collectibles**
6 Homerton Street
Cambridge CB2 8NX
+44(0)1223 240333
www.innersanctumcollectibles.com

**The Magic Joke Shop**
29 Bridge Street
Cambridge CB2 1UJ
+44 (0)1223 353003
www.jokeshop.co.uk

## LEATHER GOODS

**Cambridge Craft Market
at All Saints Garden** 36
All Saints Garden
Trinity Street
Cambridge CB2 1TQ
+44 (0)7769 628788
www.cambridge-craft-market.co.uk

**Cambridge Satchel
Company Ltd**
+44(0)1223 833050
www.cambridgesatchel.co.uk

**General and
Sunday Markets** 76
Market Square
Cambridge CB2
+44 (0)1223 457000
www.cambridge.gov.uk/markets

**Ian Stevens**
28 Magdalene Street
Cambridge CB3 0AF
+44 (0)1223 304100
www.ianstevenscambridge.co.uk

## LEISURE AND HOBBIES

**ADC Theatre**
Park Street
Cambridge CB5 8AS
+44 (0)1223 300085
www.adctheatre.com

**Arts Picturehouse**
38-39 St Andrews Street
Cambridge CB2 3AR
+44 (0)871 902 5720
www.picturehouses.co.uk

**Cambridge 105**
+44 (0)1223 967105
www.cambridge105.fm

**Cambridge Arts Theatre**
6 St Edwards Passage
Cambridge CB2 3PJ
+44 (0)1223 503333
www.cambridgeartstheatre.com

**Cambridge Cookery School**
Unit 9D
The Imre Building
Homerton Business Centre
Purbeck Road
Cambridge CB2 8HN
+44 (0)1223 247620
www.cambridgecookeryschool.com

**Cambridge Coral Tech**
160 Blinco Grove
Cambridge CB1 7TT
+44 (0)1223 413243
www.cambridgecoraltech.co.uk

**The Cambridge Stamp Centre**
29 Hobson Street
Cambridge CB1 1NL
+44 (0)1223 363980
www.cambridgecovers.co.uk

**Campkins Camera Centre**
11 Rose Crescent
Cambridge CB2 3LP
+44 (0)1223 364223
www.campkinscameras.co.uk

**Fitzwilliam Museum**
Trumpington Street
Cambridge CB2 1RB
+44 (0)1223 332900
www.fitzmuseum.cam.ac.uk

**Folk Museum**                     14
2/3 Castle Street
Cambridge CB3 0AQ
+44 (0)1223 355159
www.folkmuseum.org.uk

**Hobbs Sports**
36 Sidney Street
Cambridge CB2 3HX
+44 (0)1223 362428
www.hobbssports.co.uk

**Inner Sanctum Collectibles**
6 Homerton Street
Cambridge CB2 8NX
+44(0)1223 240333
www.innersanctumcollectibles.com

**Kettle's Yard**                   12
Castle Street
Cambridge CB3 0AQ
+44 (0)1223 748100
www.kettlesyard.co.uk

**Open Air**                        50
11 Green Street
Cambridge CB2 3JU
+44 (0)1223 324666
www.openair.co.uk

**Scudamore's Punting Company Ltd**
Granta Place, Mill Lane
Cambridge CB2 1RS
+44 (0)1223 359 750
www.scudamores.com

**The Sheep Shop**
72 Beche Road
Cambridge CB5 8HU
+44 (0)1223 311268
www.sheepshopcambridge.co.uk

**St Barnabas Press**               132
Coldhams Road
Cambridge CB1 3EW
+44 (0)1223 413792
stbarnabaspress.webplus.net

**White House Arts**                124
72 Fen Road
Cambridge CB4 1UN
+44 (0)1223 420018
www.whitehousearts.co.uk

## MUSIC/MUSICAL INSTRUMENTS

**Brennan**
www.brennan.co.uk

**Cambridge Strings**               64
72 King Street
Cambridge CB1 1LN
+44(0)1223 323388
www.cambridgestrings.co.uk

**Millers Music Centre & Ken Stevens**
12 Sussex Street
Cambridge CB1 1PW
+44 (0)1223 354452 /367758
www.millersmusic.co.uk

**Richard Wilson Bow Maker**        100
The Workshop
36 Kingston Street
Cambridge CB1 2NU
+44 (0)1223 354115
www.bowmaker.co.uk

**Woolston Violins**               114
222 Mill Road
Cambridge CB1 3NF
+44 (0)1223 413860
www.woolstonviolins.com

## OPTICIANS AND EYEWEAR

**Clamp Optometrists**
7 St. Andrew's Street
Cambridge CB2 3AX
+44 (0)1223 350043
www.clampoptometrists.com

**Eyelink**
23 Hills Rd, Cambridge CB23 5RT
+44 (0)1223 315226
www.eyelinkcambridge.co.uk

**Taank Optometrists** 96
92A Mill Road
Cambridge CB1 2BD
+44 (0)1223 350071
www.taankoptometrists.co.uk

## PETS

**Cambridge Coral Tech**
160 Blinco Grove
Cambridge CB1 7TT
+44 (0)1223 413243
www.cambridgecoraltech.co.uk

**Grumpy's Pets**
150a Scotland Road
Cambridge CB4 1QQ
+44 (0)1223 566488
www.grumpypets.co.uk

## PICTURE FRAMING

**Cambridge Framing Centre**
20 Sussex Street
Cambridge CB1 1PA
+44 (0)1223 300711
www.cambridgeframingcentre.co.uk

**Frameworks** 104
170 Mill Road
Cambridge CB1 3LP
+44 (0)1223 213092/778817
www.frameworks-cambridge.co.uk

**The Lawson Gallery**
7/8 King's Parade
Cambridge CB2 1SJ
+44 (0)1223 313970
www.lawson-gallery.com

**Makers' Gallery**
3-4 Hope Street Yard, Mill Road
Cambridge CB1 3NA
+44 (0)1223 414870
www.makersgallery.co.uk

## PUBS, BARS AND CLUBS

**12a Club**
12a Market Hill
Cambridge CB2 3NJ
+44 (0)1223 350106
www.12aclub.com

**196**
196 Mill Road, Cambridge CB1 3NF

**The Blue Ball** 148
57 Broadway, Grantchester
Cambridge CB3 9NQ
+44 (0)1223 840679

**The Cambridge Blue**
85-87 Gwydir Street
Cambridge CB1 2LG
+44 (0)1223 471680
www.the-cambridgeblue.co.uk

**The Clarendon Arms**
35-36 Clarendon Street
Cambridge CB1 1JX
+44 (0)1223 971015
www.clarendoncambridge.com

**De Luca**
83 Regent Street
Cambridge CB2 1AW
+44 (0)1223 356666
www.delucacucina.co.uk

**The Devonshire Arms**
1 Devonshire Road
Cambridge CB1 2BH
+44 (0)1223 316610
www.individualpubs.co.uk

**Hidden Rooms**
7a Jesus Lane
Cambridge CB5 8BA
+44 (0)1223 514777
www.cubender.com/
hidden_rooms

**Kingston Arms Freehouse**
33 Kingston Street
Cambridge CB1 2NU
+44 (0)1223 319414
www.kingston-arms.co.uk

**La Raza** 72
4-6 Rose Crescent
Cambridge CB2 3LL
+44 (0)1223 464550
www.laraza.co.uk

**Live and Let Live**
40 Mawson Road
Cambridge CB1 2EA
+44 (0)1223 460261
www.the-live.co.uk

**The Maypole**
20A Portugal Place
Cambridge CB5 8AF
+44 (0)1223 352999
www.maypolefreehouse.co.uk

**Ta Bouche** 70
10-15 Market Passage
Cambridge CB2 3PF
+44(0)1223 462277
www.tabouche.co.uk

## RESTAURANTS

**Al Casbah**
62 Mill Road
Cambridge CB1 2AS
+44 (0)1223 579500/561666
www.al-casbah.com

**Alimentum**
152-154 Hills Road
Cambridge CB2 8PB
+44 (0)1223 413000
www.restaurantalimentum.co.uk

**Backstreet Bistro**
Sturton Street
Cambridge CB1 2QA
+44(0)1223 306306

**Bibimbap House**
60 Mill Road
Cambridge CB1 2AS
+44 (0)1223 506800

**Cambridge Chop House**
1 King's Parade
Cambridge CB2 1SJ
+44(0)1223 359506
www.cambscuisine.com

**CB2**
5/7 Norfolk Street
Cambridge CB1 2LD
+44 (0)1223 508503
www.cb2bistro.com

**Cotto**
183 East Road
Cambridge CB1 1BG
+44(0)1223 302010
www.cottocambridge.co.uk

**De Luca**
83 Regent Street
Cambridge CB2 1AW
+44 (0)1223 356666
www.delucacucina.co.uk

**Don Pasquale** 74
12 Market Hill
Cambridge CB2 3NJ
+44 (0)1223 367063
www.donpasquale.co.uk

**Efes**
80 King Street
Cambridge CB1 1LN
+44 (0)1223 500005
www.efesrestaurant-cambridge.co.uk

**Eraina**
2 Free School Lane
Cambridge CB2 3QA
+44 (0)1223 368786

**Fitzbillies** 90
52 Trumpington Street
Cambridge CB2 1RG
+44 (0)1223 352500
www.fitzbillies.com

**Galleria Restaurant**
33 Bridge Street
Cambridge CB2 1UW
+44 (0)1223 362054
www.galleriacambridge.co.uk

**Graffiti /Hotel Felix**
Whitehouse Lane
Huntingdon Road
Cambridge CB3 0LX
+44(0)1223 277977
www.hotelfelix.co.uk

**Kymmoy**
11 Burleigh Street
Cambridge CB1 1DG
www.kymmoy.co.uk

**La Margherita**
15 Magdalene Street
Cambridge CB3 0AF
+44 (0)1223 315232
www.lamargheritacambridge.com

**La Raza** 72
4-6 Rose Crescent
Cambridge CB2 3LL
+44(0)1223 464550
www.laraza.co.uk

**Le Gros Franck** 142
57 Hills Road
Cambridge CB2 1NT
+44 (0)1223 565560
www.legrosfranck.com

**Midsummer House**
Midsummer Common
Cambridge CB4 1HA
+44 (0)1223 369299
www.midsummerhouse.co.uk

**The Oak Bistro**
6 Lensfield Road
Cambridge CB2 1EG
+44 (0)1223 323361
www.theoakbistro.co.uk

**The Punter**
3 Pound Hill
Cambridge CB3 0AE
+44 (0)1223 363322
www.thepuntercambridge.com

**Rainbow Cafe**
9a King's Parade
Cambridge CB2 1SJ
+44 (0)1223 321551
www.rainbowcafe.co.uk

**Restaurant 22**
22 Chesterton Road
Cambridge CB4 3AX
+44 (0)1223 351880
www.restaurant22.co.uk

**Sala Thong**
35 Newnham Road
Cambridge CB3 9EY
+44 (0)1223 323178
www.salathong.co.uk

**The Sea Tree** 108
13/14 The Broadway, Mill Road
Cambridge CB1 3AH
+44 (0)1223 414349
www.theseatree.co.uk

**St John's Chop House** 16
21-24 Northampton Street
Cambridge CB3 0AD
+44 (0)1223 353110
www.cambscuisine.com

**Ta Bouche** 70
10-15 Market Passage
Cambridge CB2 3PF
+44(0)1223 462277
www.tabouche.co.uk

**Thanh Binh**
17 Magdalene Street
Cambridge CB3 0AF
+44 (0)1223 362456
www.thanhbinh.co.uk

**The Varsity Hotel & Spa**  30
Thompson's Lane (off Bridge St)
Cambridge CB5 8AQ
+44 (0)1223 306030
www.thevarsityhotel.co.uk

**Yippee Noodle Bar**  60
7-9 King Street
Cambridge CB1 1LH
+44 (0)1223 518111
www.yippeenoodlebar.co.uk

## TAKEAWAY FOOD

**Inder's Kitchen**  156
+44 (0)1223 211333
www.inderskitchen.com

## TATTOOING

**Tattooing by Fabio**
96a Mill Road
Cambridge CB1 2BD
+44 (0)1223 354299
www.tattooingbyfabio.com

## WINE AND BEER

**Bacchanalia**  126
79 Victoria Road
Cambridge CB4 3BS
+44 (0)1223 576292
www.winegod.co.uk
(also Mill Road)

**BlackBar Brewery**
Unit B3
Button End Industrial Estate
Harston, Cambridge CB22 7GX
+44 (0)1223 872131
www.blackbar.co.uk

**Burwash Manor**
New Road, Barton
Cambridge CB23 7EY
www.burwashmanor.com

**Cambridge Wine Merchants**
42 Mill Road
Cambridge CB1 2AD
+44 (0)1223 568993
www.cambridgewine.com
(also Bridge Street, Kings
Parade, Cherry Hinton Road)

**Chilford Hall Vineyard**
Balsham Road
Linton CB21 4LE
+44 (0)1223 895600
www.chilfordhall.co.uk

**Fellows Brewery Ltd**
2 Leopold Walk, Cottenham
Cambridge CB24 8XS
+44 (0)1954 250262
www.fellowsbrewery.co.uk

**The Milton Brewery, Cambridge Ltd**
Pegasus House
Pembroke Avenue
Waterbeach
Cambridge CB25 9PY
+44 (0)1223 862067
www.miltonbrewery.co.uk

**Moonshine Brewery**
Shelford Road, Fulbourn
Cambridge CB21 5EQ
+44 (0)7906 066794
www.moonshinebrewery.co.uk

**Noel Young**
56 High Street, Trumpington
Cambridge CB2 9LS
+44 (0)1223 566744
www.nywines.co.uk

## About PHL Publishing Limited

In 2010, a think-tank voted Cambridge 'number one clone town'. In its report *Reimaging the High Street*, The New Economics Foundation called our city centre a 'clone zone' – with a bland and homogenous offering. Although this is true in some areas of Cambridge, we wanted to prove that this is only part of the story. Alongside the usual chain stores and often in the most beautiful and historic areas of the City, there are some fantastic independents – doing things their way and doing them extremely well.

*Andrew Houston, Steve Linford, Anne Prince.*

As long term residents of the City and avid supporters of independents, we decided to form our own independent publishing company. This allowed us to combine our writing, photography and design skills to produce *Independent Cambridge* – a celebration of the diversity and individuality unique to 'indies'.

In our travels we have discovered many more fantastic independents right across the City and beyond, embracing an even wider range of people and places. In addition to shops, restaurants, cafes, bars, galleries and hotels, we have found an incredible number of crafts people, artists, courses, independents on the web and individuals offering professional services.

Starting out as avid independent supporters we've become just a little bit obsessed!